Keynote

2A COMBO SPLIT

David Bohlke
Eunice Yeates

NATIONAL GEOGRAPHIC LEARNING | CENGAGE Learning

Australia • Brazil • Mexico • Singapore • United Kingdom • United States

NATIONAL GEOGRAPHIC LEARNING | CENGAGE Learning

Keynote Combo Split 2A
David Bohlke and Eunice Yeates

Publisher: Andrew Robinson
Executive Editor: Sean Bermingham
Senior Development Editor: Derek Mackrell
Development Editor: Christopher Street
Director of Global Marketing: Ian Martin
Senior Product Marketing Manager: Caitlin Thomas
IP Analyst: Kyle Cooper
IP Project Manager: Carissa Poweleit
Media Researcher: Leila Hishmeh
Senior Director of Production: Michael Burggren
Senior Production Controller: Tan Jin Hock
Manufacturing Planner: Mary Beth Hennebury
Compositor: SPi Global
Cover/Text Design: Brenda Carmichael
Cover Photo: The Park Royal Hotel green terrace in Singapore: © Patrick Bingham Hall

Combo Split 2A with My Keynote Online:
ISBN-13: 978-1-337-10894-2

Combo Split 2A:
ISBN-13: 978-1-337-10878-2

National Geographic Learning
20 Channel Center Street
Boston, MA 02210
USA

Cengage Learning is a leading provider of customized learning solutions with office locations around the globe, including Singapore, the United Kingdom, Australia, Mexico, Brazil, and Japan. Locate your local office at **international.cengage.com/region**

Cengage Learning products are represented in Canada by Nelson Education, Ltd.

Visit National Geographic Learning online at **NGL.cengage.com**
Visit our corporate website at **www.cengage.com**

Printed in the United States of America
Print Number: 01 Print Year: 2017

Contents

Featured TEDTALKS

1 Munir Virani
Why I love vultures

2 A. J. Jacobs
The world's largest family reunion

3 Ann Morgan
My year reading a book from every country

4 Daria van den Bercken
Why I take the piano on the road … and in the air

5 Roman Mars
The worst-designed thing you've never noticed

6 Jarrett J. Krosoczka
How a boy became an artist

Scope and Sequence

	LESSON A		LESSON B	
UNIT	**VOCABULARY**	**LISTENING**	**LANGUAGE FOCUS**	**SPEAKING**
1  **Protectors**	Types of animals	**Moving people to action** *Joel Sartore, photographer*	**Function** Describing events in the present **Grammar** Simple present and present continuous	Protecting species
2  **Family Connections**	Extended family	**My family history** *Ken Lejtenyi, sales director*	**Function** Talking about future plans **Grammar** Future forms	My family
3  **Global Stories**	Genres of fiction	**Interview with an author** *Madeleine Thien, author*	**Function** Adding details **Grammar** Relative clauses	Can you guess?
	PRESENTATION 1 Talking about an endangered species			
4  **Music**	Music	**A traditional singer** *Iarla Ó Lionáird, singer*	**Function** Talking about quantity **Grammar** Countable and uncountable nouns	Musical preferences
5  **Good Design**	Design elements	**A designer's advice** *Sarah Lafferty, designer*	**Function** Talking about place and position **Grammar** Prepositions of place	Designing a coat of arms
6  **Inspiration**	Sources of inspiration	**My inspiration** *Franklin Chang Diaz, former astronaut*	**Function** Reporting what someone said **Grammar** Reported speech	Getting advice
	PRESENTATION 2 Describing a favorite teacher			

LESSON C	LESSON D		LESSON E	
READING	**TED TALK**	**PRESENTATION SKILLS**	**COMMUNICATE**	**WRITING**
Vultures in danger	**WHY I LOVE VULTURES** *Munir Virani*	Signposting with questions	A group decision	Writing about an endangered species
Genealogy	**THE WORLD'S LARGEST FAMILY REUNION** *A. J. Jacobs*	Personalizing a presentation	Family tree	Writing an invitation
Top picks	**MY YEAR READING A BOOK FROM EVERY COUNTRY** *Ann Morgan*	Closing a presentation	A book recommendation	Writing a book review
Music and the brain	**WHY I TAKE THE PIANO ON THE ROAD ... AND IN THE AIR** *Daria van den Bercken*	Providing background information	Desert island discs	Writing about a favorite song
Symbol of a city	**THE WORST-DESIGNED THING YOU'VE NEVER NOTICED** *Roman Mars*	Numbering key points	A new city flag	Writing about your country's flag
Inspiring lives	**HOW A BOY BECAME AN ARTIST** *Jarrett Krosoczka*	Using your voice effectively	A lively dinner party	Writing about an inspiring person

Welcome to Keynote!

In this book, you will develop your English language skills and explore great ideas with an authentic TED Talk. Each unit topic is based around a TED speaker's main idea.

In Unit 4, Daria van den Bercken encourages people to discover and appreciate the wonder of music.

LISTENING AND SPEAKING

- Practice listening to real people talking about the unit topic. Real-life people featured in this book include an author, a singer, and a designer.
- Develop your **speaking confidence** with a model conversation and guided speaking tasks.

See pages 47, 49

VOCABULARY AND GRAMMAR

- In each unit, you'll learn key words, phrases, and grammar structures for talking about the unit topic.
- Build **language and visual literacy skills** with real-life information—in Unit 4, you'll learn about the best kinds of music for various activities.

See page 48

READING

- Develop your **reading and vocabulary skills** with a specially adapted reading passage. In Unit 4, you'll learn about the effects of music on the brain.
- The passage includes several words and phrases that appear later in the TED Talk.

See pages 50–51

VIEWING

- Practice your viewing and **critical thinking** skills as you watch a specially adapted TED Talk.
- Notice how TED speakers use effective language and **communication** skills to present their ideas.

See pages 52–53

COMMUNICATING AND PRESENTING

- Use your **creativity** and **collaboration skills** in a final task that reviews language and ideas from the unit.

See page 54

- Build your **speaking confidence** further in a Presentation task (after every three units).

See page 75

WRITING

- Communicate your own ideas about the unit topic in a controlled writing task.

See page 54

- Develop your **writing and language skills** further in the **Keynote Workbook** and online at **MyKeynoteOnline**.

What is TED?

TED has a simple goal: to spread great ideas. Every year, hundreds of presenters share ideas at TED events around the world. Millions of people watch TED Talks online. The talks inspire many people to change their attitudes and their lives.

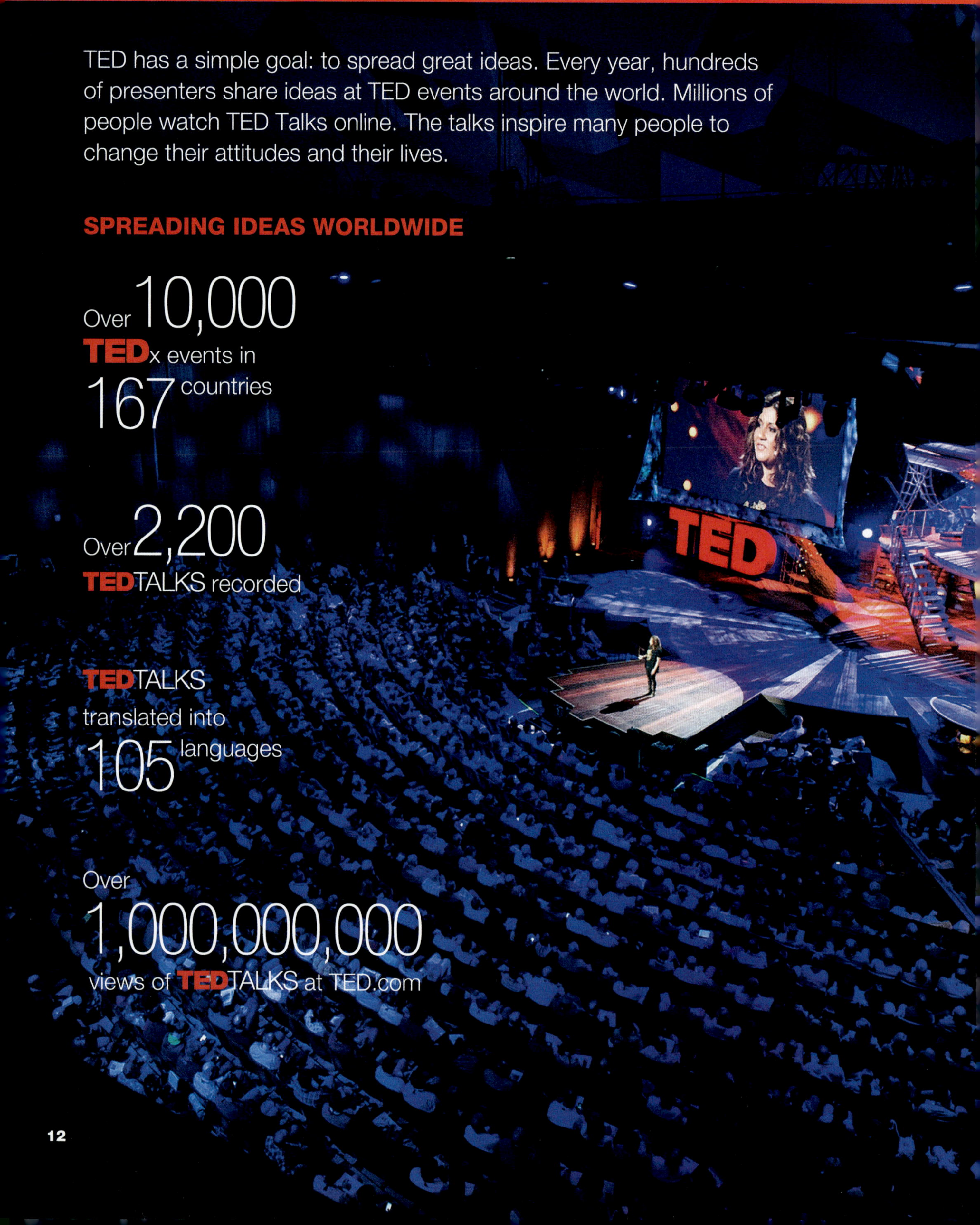

SPREADING IDEAS WORLDWIDE

Over 10,000 TEDx events in 167 countries

Over 2,200 TEDTALKS recorded

TEDTALKS translated into 105 languages

Over 1,000,000,000 views of TEDTALKS at TED.com

1 Protectors

Munir Virani
Biologist, TED speaker

UNIT GOALS

In this unit, you will ...

- talk about endangered and threatened animals.
- read about why vulture numbers are declining.
- watch a TED Talk about the importance of saving vultures.

WARM UP

▶ **1.1** Watch part of Munir Virani's TED Talk. Answer the questions with a partner.

1 Why do you think vultures are threatened?

2 What's your impression of vultures? Do you agree with Virani?

A critically endangered Indochinese box turtle photographed by Joel Sartore as part of his Photo Ark project

1A Animals under threat

VOCABULARY Types of animals

A Read the paragraph about Joel Sartore's Photo Ark project. Complete the table with the words in **bold**.

Joel Sartore's Photo Ark project started with endangered **amphibians**. Sartore wanted to do something to show these species to the world before they were gone forever. Soon, Sartore heard about other species in trouble—**mammals, reptiles, birds, fish, insects**. Now, he photographs anything that will stay still long enough for him to take a photo.

Amphibians					
frogs toads	turtles crocodiles	butterflies ants	owls flamingos	sharks tuna	tigers pandas

B Work with a partner. Add one more animal to each of the categories in the table.

C What animals do you know that are endangered? Discuss with a partner.

I think most species of tigers are endangered.

Yeah, I think you're right.

LISTENING Moving people to action

Listening for gist
When you listen to something for the first time, just focus on the speaker's overall message. Listen again for more details.

A ▶ 1.2 Watch photographer Joel Sartore talking about the Photo Ark. What does he mean when he talks about "moving people to action?"

Photographer Joel Sartore

B ▶ 1.2 Watch again. Complete the sentences with the words you hear.

1 "My goal is to get people to wake up and say 'Whoa! That's ___________!'"

2 "I shoot ___________ pictures a year, minimum."

3 "Maybe ___________ are keepers."

C **CRITICAL THINKING**

Evaluating Do you agree that photographs can "move people to action?" Discuss with a partner.

SPEAKING Talking about endangered animals

A ▶ 1.3 What is the biggest threat to the Sumatran elephant?

A: Hey! Check out these elephants.

B: Cool! Are they African elephants?

A: No, they're Sumatran elephants. Oh, how awful. It says here that they are facing extinction. — are endangered / could become extinct

B: That's terrible. Does it say why?

A: Um … it's mostly because people are cutting down the rain forest. But another reason is that people illegally hunt and kill them. — illegal hunting / poaching

B: How many are there in the wild? — remain / still live

A: Let's see … between 2,400 and 2,800.

B: They're such beautiful animals. I really hope people can find a way to save them. — help / protect

B Practice the conversation with a partner. Practice again using the words on the right.

C Work with a partner to make notes about an endangered animal. Join another pair and share your information.

Animal	Where do they live?	Why are they endangered?

Mountain gorillas live in Africa.

Yeah, and they're endangered because they're losing their habitat.

1B How we're helping

LANGUAGE FOCUS Discussing conservation status

A ▶ 1.4 Read the information. Why do you think reindeer populations are healthy?

RISKS OF EXTINCTION

Many animals are facing threats to their survival. The International Union for Conservation of Nature uses a scale to track the conservation status of our world's animal species.

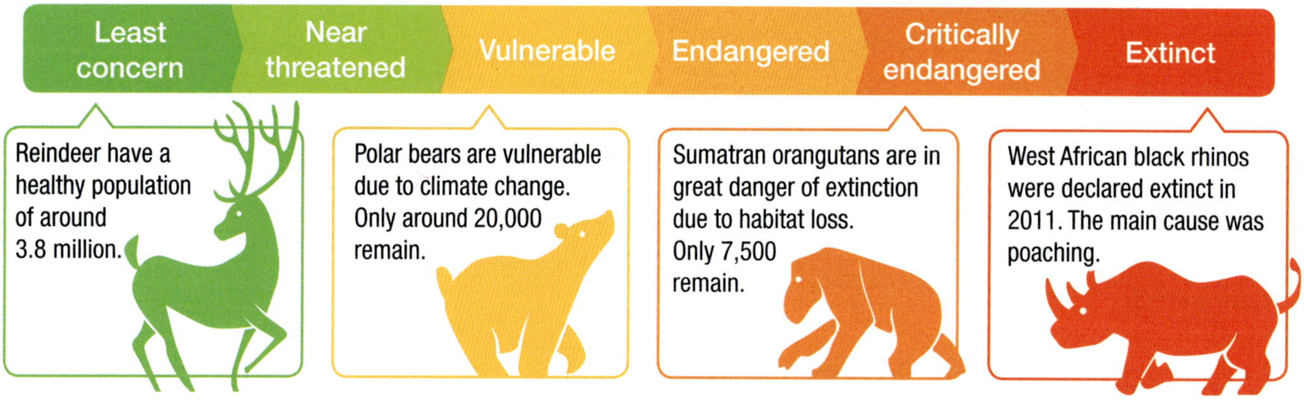

B ▶ 1.5 Listen to an expert talk about three species of fish. Write the conservation status of each one.

1 barracuda: ______ **2** bigeye tuna: ______ **3** silver trout: ______

C ▶ 1.6 Watch and study the language in the chart.

Describing events in the present	
Every year, the Arctic freezes and melts. Polar bears live in the Arctic. Polar bears hunt seals. Does a vulnerable species have any living individuals? Does an extinct species have any living individuals?	 Yes, it does. No, it doesn't.
Our planet's temperature is rising. Polar bears are now losing their hunting grounds. These days, polar bear numbers are declining. Is the world's climate changing? Is the Earth's temperature falling? Why are polar bear numbers decreasing?	 Yes, it is. No, it isn't. Because it's harder for them to hunt seals.

For more information on **simple present** and **present continuous**, see Grammar Summary 1 on page 155.

D Match each question to the best response.

1 Do orangutans live in Southeast Asia?	○	○ Yes, it does.
2 Where do they spend most of their time?	○	○ Yes, they do.
3 Are their numbers declining?	○	○ They're trying to protect the forests.
4 Why are the numbers dropping?	○	○ They usually live in trees.
5 What are people doing to protect them?	○	○ It's mainly because of habitat loss.
6 Does poaching threaten them, too?	○	○ Yes, they are.

E Circle the correct words.

1 The green sea turtle (**gets / is getting**) its name from the color of its skin.

2 On average, they (**live / are living**) up to 80 years.

3 Every year, they (**lay / are laying**) thousands of eggs on Florida's beaches.

4 Because of laws protecting their nesting sites, their numbers (**rise / are rising**).

5 The U.S. Fish and Wildlife Service (**considers / is considering**) changing their status from endangered to threatened.

F ▶ 1.7 Complete the information with the correct form of the words in the box. Listen and check your answers.

do	have	kill	(not) hurt	rise	(not) want

Every year, poachers [1]__________ over 1,000 rhinos in southern Africa. They hunt them for their horns because some people believe the horns [2]__________ special medicinal value. The Rhino Rescue Project [3]__________ something about it. They are able to make the horn lose its value. But how?

They inject a poison into the horns of living animals. The poison [4]__________ the rhino, but it makes the horn useless as medicine. Consumers [5]__________ horns that can make them feel sick. These actions are working. Rhino numbers [6]__________ slowly.

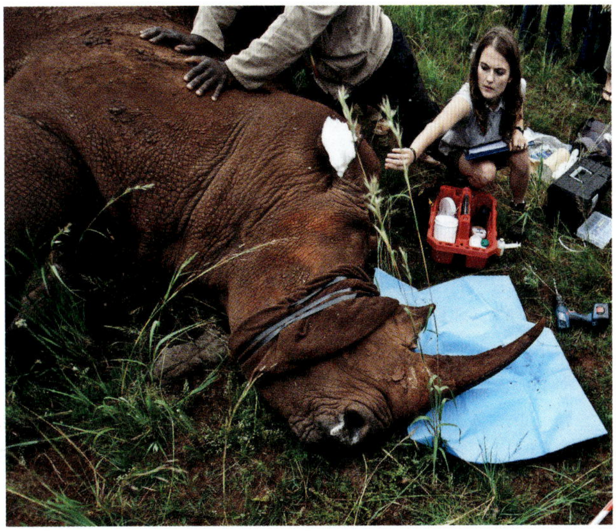

SPEAKING Protecting species

A Work with a partner. What do you know about these two animal species?

Bengal tigers	kiwis

B You are going to learn about these species. **Student A**: Turn to page 141. **Student B**: Turn to page 142.

Without protection, many believe vultures could soon be extinct.

1C Vultures in danger

PRE-READING Predicting

Discuss with a partner. Why do you think vultures might be in danger? Check your ideas as you read the passage.

1.8

1 In the early 1990s, something began to happen to India's vultures. Once, tens of millions of these birds filled the skies. Then, suddenly, they began to die out. In less than a decade, the three most common Indian vulture species declined by more than 95 percent. The Oriental white-backed vulture population—once the most common large bird of prey[1] in the world—fell by an incredible 99.9 percent. It was one of the fastest population collapses of any bird species in history.

2 Scientists eventually traced the cause of the decline to a pain-killing drug called diclofenac, which was used to **treat** sick livestock. Although safe for cows, it is deadly to vultures. Any vulture feeding on the flesh[2] of a cow treated with diclofenac soon becomes ill. Millions of vultures died as a result. To stop the decline, India's **government** banned the drug's use on animals in 2006. Today, the country's vulture decline is slowing.

3 Conservationists are now **worried** something similar may be happening in Africa. The continent has already lost one of its eleven vulture species, and seven others are endangered. As with India, a major threat is poisoning. In rural **communities**, it is **common** for herders to lose cows and other livestock to predators. When a lion attacks and kills a cow, the farmers often put poison in the cow's carcass.[3] This kills the lion when it returns to feed. However, vultures also die from the poison when they feed off a poisoned carcass. Researchers believe this may be the cause of over 60 percent of vulture deaths across Africa.

4 Hopefully, Africa can learn from India's recent successes. Vultures may not be cute, say conservationists, but they are one of nature's most important scavengers.[4] Without protection, Africa's vultures may be extinct within the next 50 to 100 years.

[1] **bird of prey:** *n.* a bird that eats other animals
[2] **flesh:** *n.* the soft part of the body between the bones and skin
[3] **carcass:** *n.* the body of a dead animal
[4] **scavenger:** *n.* an animal that eats dead animals or plants

UNDERSTANDING GIST

According to the passage, which of these best describes vultures?

- **a** birds that spread diseases
- **b** endangered birds that need our help
- **c** the African lion's best friend
- **d** the strangest of all bird species

UNDERSTANDING MAIN IDEAS

Match the paragraph with the main question it answers. One question is extra.

1 Paragraph 1 ○	○	Why are vulture numbers in Africa declining?
2 Paragraph 2 ○	○	Why did vulture populations decline in India?
3 Paragraph 3 ○	○	Why is it important to protect Africa's vultures?
4 Paragraph 4 ○	○	What will happen to India's vultures in the future?
	○	What happened to India's vultures in the 1990s?

UNDERSTANDING CAUSE AND EFFECT

Why have vulture numbers declined? Use the sentences (**a–f**) to complete the summary.

- **a** A farmer places poison inside a cow's dead body.
- **b** People give a drug to sick cows.
- **c** Vultures eventually die due to diclofenac poisoning.
- **d** Both lions and vultures feed on a cow, and they die from poisoning.
- **e** A lion attacks and kills a cow, so the herder decides to kill the lion.
- **f** Vultures start to get sick after they feed on a cow treated with medicine.

India: ______ → ______ → ______ **Africa:** ______ → ______ → ______

BUILDING VOCABULARY

A Match each word in **blue** from the passage to its definition.

1 **treat** ○	○	the group of people who control a country
2 **worried** ○	○	usual; happening often
3 **common** ○	○	thinking about future problems
4 **community** ○	○	a group of people who live in the same area
5 **government** ○	○	to try to make a sick person or animal well again

B **CRITICAL THINKING**

Reflecting Discuss the questions with a partner.

1. What might be some ways to protect the vultures in Africa?
2. What are some other ways farmers could protect their cows instead of using poison?

1D Why I love vultures

TEDTALKS

Biologist **MUNIR VIRANI** does not want people to think of vultures as **greedy** or ugly **creatures**. Instead, he wants people to understand the **ecological** services they provide. His idea worth spreading is that vultures are **vital** to the environment and to human health, and deserve to be protected.

PREVIEWING

Read the paragraph above. Match each **bold** word to its meaning. You will hear these words in the TED Talk.

1 extremely important: ________________

2 animals of any type: ________________

3 environmental: ________________

4 wanting more than needed: ________________

VIEWING

A ▶ **1.9** Watch Part 1 of the TED Talk. Complete the notes.

Generally viewed negatively by society	Two types	Importance of vultures
• Darwin described turkey vultures as "disgusting birds." • Disney has often portrayed vultures as [1]____________ characters.	• New World vultures: mainly found in [2]____________ • Old World vultures: [3]____________ out of 16 species are at high risk of extinction	• clean up animal carcasses and help control the spread of [4]____________

B ▶ **1.10** Watch Part 2 of the TED Talk. Circle the correct option to complete each sentence.

1 People are doing research to find out (**where vultures go** / **what vultures eat**).

2 Virani says that saving vultures is a(n) (**local** / **international**) problem.

3 Virani says we can all help by (**visiting zoos to learn** / **educating people**) about vultures.

4 Darwin changed his mind about vultures when he watched them (**fly** / **clean up a carcass**).

C **CRITICAL THINKING**

Reflecting Has your opinion of vultures changed after watching Virani's TED Talk? Discuss with a partner.

TEDTALKS

VOCABULARY IN CONTEXT

▶ 1.11 Watch the excerpts from the TED Talk. Choose the correct meaning of the words.

PRESENTATION SKILLS Signposting with questions

One useful way to organize a presentation is to begin each major part by asking the audience a question. This helps the audience know exactly what you are going to talk about.

A ▶ 1.12 Watch the excerpt. Complete the question Virani asked near the start of his presentation.

"First of all, ______________________ such a bad press?"

B ▶ 1.13 Match the questions Virani asks with the responses he gives. Watch and check your answers.

1 So why are vultures important? ○	○ You can become active, make noise.
2 So what is the problem with vultures? ○	○ First of all, they provide vital ecological services.
3 So what's being done? ○	○ Well, we're conducting research on these birds.
4 How can you help? ○	○ We have eight species of vultures that occur in Kenya of which six are highly threatened with extinction

C Imagine you are going to give a presentation on pandas. Write three key points about them. Then exchange notes with a partner. Write a signposting question for each key point.

Key points	**Questions**
1 ______________________.	______________________?
2 ______________________.	______________________?
3 ______________________.	______________________?

A palm-nut vulture in flight, Bioko Island, Equatorial Guinea

1E Which to save?

COMMUNICATE A group decision

A Work with a partner. Look at the photos of endangered species below. Guess the names of the animals.

Indian ___________

Frégate Island ___________

bluefin ___________

marine ___________

B Work in groups of four. You are members of an organization that raises money to protect endangered species. **Student A:** Turn to page 141. **Student B:** Turn to page 142. **Student C:** Turn to page 144. **Student D:** Turn to page 146. Read the information and make notes about your animal.

C Your organization only has enough money to help save one animal. Use your notes and take turns presenting the information you learned about your animal to your group. Then, work together to choose the one animal you are going to save.

> **Presenting arguments**
> *For one thing ...* *Something else to consider is ...* *The most important thing is ...*

D Compare your group's decision with others in the class. Which animal was most popular? Why do you think this was the case?

WRITING An endangered species

Write about an animal you think needs protection.

> An animal that needs our protection is the polar bear. Rising sea levels are threatening its survival. We have a responsibility to save polar bears because humans caused climate change.

2 Family Connections

"All of you have famous people and historical figures in your tree, because we are all connected ..."

A. J. Jacobs
Writer, TED speaker

UNIT GOALS

In this unit, you will ...

- talk about your immediate and extended family.
- read about researching family trees.
- watch a TED Talk about how we are all connected.

WARM UP

2.1 Watch part of A. J. Jacobs's TED Talk. Answer the questions with a partner.

1 What does Jacobs mean when he says, "we are all connected"?

2 What do you think is the importance of a world family tree?

A family reunites at a Christmas party.

2A Family ties

VOCABULARY Extended family

A 2.2 Look at the family tree. Complete the sentences using the words in the box. Listen and check your answers.

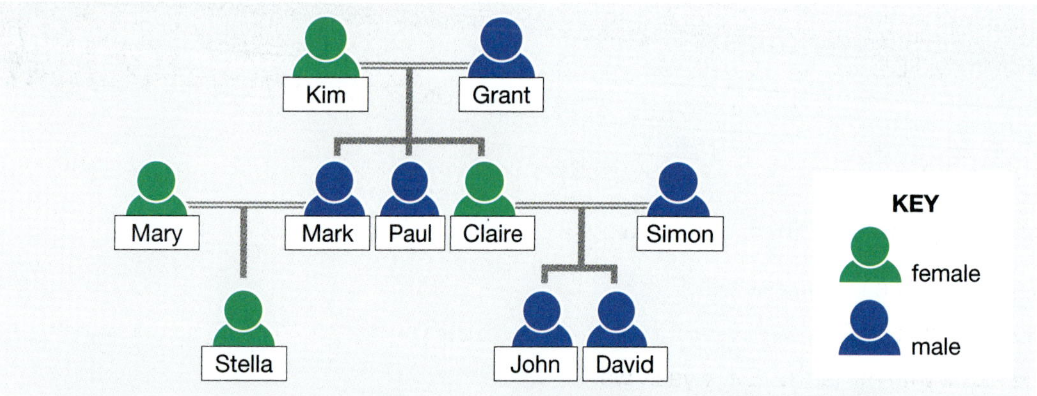

brother-in-law	cousin	grandchild	grandfather
mother-in-law	nephew	niece	son-in-law

1 Kim is Mary's ______________________.

2 Stella is John's ______________________.

3 Grant is John's ______________________.

4 Simon is Kim's ______________________.

5 John is Grant's ______________________.

6 Simon is Paul's ______________________.

7 Stella is Claire's ______________________.

8 David is Mark's ______________________.

B Work with a partner. Describe a connection to someone in your family. Your partner must name the relationship.

Joanna is my mother's father's mother.

Is she your great-grandmother?

LISTENING My family history

Listening for contractions versus possessives
When we hear "**'s**" after a noun of a person's name, it might be a contraction of *is* or a possessive form. Listen carefully to be sure you catch the right meaning.
Contraction of *is*: *John's 21 years old.*
Possessive form: *John's cousin is 21 years old.*

A ▶ **2.3** Watch Ken Lejtenyi talking about his family history. Circle the countries that he mentions.

Canada	England	France	Hungary
Italy	Romania	Scotland	Singapore

B ▶ **2.3** Watch again. Complete the sentences with a country from **A**.

1. Lejtenyi's mother's parents moved to Canada from ____________.
2. His mother was born in ____________.
3. His father's parents met in ____________.
4. His father grew up in ____________.

Ken Lejtenyi and his wife at an ice hockey game in Canada

C **CRITICAL THINKING**

Reflecting Do you think many Canadians have an international family history like Lejtenyi? Discuss with a partner.

SPEAKING Talking about family

A ▶ **2.4** Where are they going to hold the family reunion? Why?

A: What are you doing for the Lunar New Year?
B: Not much. How about you? Do you have any plans? — What are you doing? / What are your plans?
A: I'm going to spend it with my family. Every year, we have a family reunion. — get-together / gathering
B: That sounds fun. Do you have a big family?
A: Yeah. My mother has seven siblings, so I have more than twenty cousins.
B: Wow! Are they all coming to your place? — house / apartment
A: Oh, no. We're going to a restaurant. Our house is way too small. — much / far
B: Well, have a good time.

B Practice the conversation with a partner. Practice again using the words on the right.

C How many people are in your immediate family? How many are in your extended family? Tell a partner.

There are five people in my immediate family—my parents, my two sisters, and me.

2B Generations

LANGUAGE FOCUS Discussing plans and arrangements

A ▶ 2.5 Read the information. Which record do you find the most amazing?

FAMILY RECORDS

The most generations alive in a single family has been seven. At 109, Augusta Bunge from the United States was the youngest living great-great-great-great-grandparent.

The highest number of children born to one mother is 69. The wife of Feodor Vassilyev from Russia (whose name is unknown) had 16 pairs of twins, seven sets of triplets, and four sets of quadruplets.

There is only one example of a family having five single children with the same birthday. Catherine (1952), Carol (1953), Charles (1956), Claudia (1961), and Cecilia Cummins (1966) were all born on 20th February.

B ▶ 2.6 Listen to someone telling his friend about some people he's going to meet this weekend. Circle the relationships.

a Chris is his (**first** / **second**) cousin. **b** Emily is Chris's (**niece** / **daughter**).

C ▶ 2.7 Watch and study the language in the chart.

Talking about future plans	
I'm leaving for the reunion on Thursday. I'm not leaving on Friday. Are you going alone? When are you coming back?	 Yes, I am. / No, I'm not. I'm coming back on Sunday.
I'm going to see my nephew this weekend. I'm not going to stay for very long. Are you going to meet your aunt and uncle? What are you going to do afterwards?	 Yes, I am. / No, I'm not. I'm going to visit a few old friends.

For more information on **future forms**, see Grammar Summary 2 on page 155.

D ▶ 2.6 Circle the correct words to complete the sentences from the conversation in **B**. Listen again to check your answers.

1 "Are you (**do**/**doing**) anything interesting this weekend?"
2 "I'm going to (**meet**/**meeting**) my second cousin."
3 "He's (**bring**/**bringing**) his daughter."
4 "I'm going to (**ask**/**asking**) Chris to help me find out more."
5 "Where are you (**meet**/**meeting**) them?"

Four generations of a family pose outside a house in Maryland, United States.

E Unscramble the questions. Then ask and answer them with a partner.

1 this weekend / seeing / are / your grandparents / you
____?

2 is going / which family member / to visit you / next
____?

3 with your family / spending / you / are / your next vacation
____?

4 you / anyone in your family / speaking with / are / this evening
____?

F ▶ 2.8 Read the paragraph. Find and correct four mistakes. Listen and check your answers.

After I finish university, I going to take a year out. I think I need a break before I start working. I'm going to travel around South America with my best friend Maki. We're meet this weekend to work out our plans. We're definitely going to start in Argentina, but we haven't decided where we're go after that. We don't have so much money so we're mainly going stay in hostels. I can't wait. It's going to be a great adventure.

SPEAKING My family

A Walk around the room and find a different person who answers *yes* to each question. For each *yes* answer, ask a follow-up question. Take notes.

Find someone who ...	Name	Extra information
is going to call a family member later today.		
is meeting a family member this weekend.		
is going on a family vacation soon.		
has both a niece and a nephew.		
is going to a wedding soon.		
has three or more siblings.		

Are you going to call a family member later today?

Yes, I am. I'm going to call my parents.

B Share the most interesting information with the class.

A woman looks through some old family photos.

2C Genealogy

PRE-READING Scanning

Work with a partner. Think of some reasons why people might search for information on their family history. Discuss your ideas. Then scan the passage to see if your ideas are mentioned.

▶ 2.9

1 Genealogy, the study of family history, is certainly nothing new. Family trees have been used for thousands of years to demonstrate claims to **wealth** and power. But the rise of the Internet has given the pursuit an explosion of new life.

2 According to some sources, genealogy is now one of the most popular topics on the Internet. Modern genealogists have a huge amount of information available online, and are able to connect with people from all around the world **with ease**. One popular ancestry website provides access to approximately 16 billion historical records. Its two million subscribers[1] have added 200 million photographs, documents, and stories to connect with 70 million family trees.

3 But what's behind our motivation to find out about our **ancestors**? Some people may have specific reasons. **Tracing** your family tree may help you reconnect with lost relatives. **Adopted** children can find out more about their birth parents. Others may want to discover a connection to a historical figure. Perhaps the most common motivation, though, is simply curiosity—a desire to better understand our place in the world. Genealogy can show our connections with people from entirely different backgrounds. As Helen Keller[2] once said, "There is no king who has not had a slave[3] among his ancestors, and no slave who has not had a king among his."

4 A. J. Jacobs's interest in genealogy started when he received an email from his twelfth cousin. Since then, Jacobs has joined one of the world's biggest family trees on Geni.com, which includes more than 75 million people. Jacobs believes that if we all realized that we're connected in this way, a lot of the problems in the world could be solved. As Jacobs says, "We're not just part of the same species. We're part of the same family."

[1] **subscriber:** *n.* someone who pays to get access to a website or to receive copies of a newspaper or magazine

[2] **Helen Keller:** *n.* an American writer, educator, and activist who was both blind and deaf

[3] **slave:** *n.* a person who is the legal property of another person

UNDERSTANDING PURPOSE

Read the passage. What is the main purpose?

a to explain the history of genealogy

b to teach the reader how to research their family tree

c to explain why people are interested in genealogy

UNDERSTANDING MAIN IDEAS

Match each paragraph to its main idea.

1 Paragraph 1 ○		○ People search for their ancestors for a variety of reasons.
2 Paragraph 2 ○		○ Genealogy could help solve problems in the world.
3 Paragraph 3 ○		○ Genealogy is very popular on the Internet.
4 Paragraph 4 ○		○ Genealogy is not new, but the Internet is changing it.

UNDERSTANDING DETAILS

Answer the questions. Circle the correct option.

1 What proof is given that genealogy is popular on the Internet?

a the number of Internet searches

b statistics from an ancestry website

2 Which of these is given as a reason for an interest in genealogy?

a to see if an ancestor had a medical condition

b to find lost family members

3 What does Helen Keller's quote mean?

a Everyone is connected to people from different backgrounds.

b People often use genealogy to show a connection to rich people.

4 Why did A. J. Jacobs become interested in genealogy?

a He found out he was related to a famous person.

b A distant relative contacted him.

BUILDING VOCABULARY

A Match each word in **blue** from the passage to its definition.

1 wealth ○		○ possession of a large amount of valuable things
2 with ease ○		○ to find or discover
3 ancestors ○		○ legally raised as your own child
4 trace ○		○ people in your family from past times
5 adopted ○		○ without difficulty

B CRITICAL THINKING

Applying To find out more about your family history, who would you talk to first? What questions would you ask? Discuss with a partner.

2D The world's largest family reunion

TEDTALKS

Writer **A. J. JACOBS** finds genealogy **fascinating**. After receiving an email from a man who claimed to be his twelfth cousin, Jacobs began planning a huge **family reunion** to meet his extended family. His idea worth spreading is that studying the world's "family tree" helps scientific progress, highlights our equality, and connects us to our **shared history** and to one another.

PREVIEWING

Read the paragraph above. Circle the correct option for each sentence below. You will hear these words in the TED Talk.

1 Something that is **fascinating** is extremely (**interesting** / **well-known**).

2 A **family reunion** is a (**gathering** / **written list**) of family members.

3 If you have **shared history** with someone, you have (**a common background** / **famous ancestors**).

VIEWING

A ▶ 2.10 Watch Part 1 of the TED Talk. Check [✓] the points Jacobs makes.

- ☐ Genealogy is undergoing a revolution partly because of genetics and the Internet.
- ☐ People can add their own information online to create and combine huge family trees.
- ☐ Putting our personal family information online can be a dangerous thing to do.
- ☐ Most people have famous people and historical figures in their family trees.

B ▶ 2.11 Watch Part 2 of the TED Talk. Jacobs gives four reasons why a world family tree is a good idea. Match each idea to a supporting detail.

Main ideas			Supporting details
1 It has scientific value.	○	○	We all come from the same ancestor.
2 It brings history alive.	○	○	We treat family better than we treat strangers.
3 It shows we are all connected.	○	○	Jacobs found out he was related to a famous person.
4 It creates a kinder world.	○	○	It provides a better understanding of human migration.

C ▶ 2.12 Watch Part 3 of the TED Talk. Complete the notes.

Event	The biggest ____________ in history
Activities	Exhibits, ________, ________, a day of ________
Who's invited?	____________

TEDTALKS

D CRITICAL THINKING

Evaluating Look back at **C**. Why do you think Jacobs wants to hold this event? Would you like to attend? Discuss with a partner.

VOCABULARY IN CONTEXT

▶ 2.13 Watch the excerpts from the TED Talk. Choose the correct meaning of the words.

PRESENTATION SKILLS Personalizing a presentation

Some speakers choose to include personal information in their presentations. Including stories about yourself, or your family members, can help engage your audience and make your presentation more "real."

A ▶ 2.14 Watch the excerpt. What does Jacobs do to personalize the presentation?

a He talks about his uncle.

b He shows a photo of a family member.

c He tells a personal story.

B Jacobs personalizes his presentation in other ways. Match the phrases below. ▶ 2.15 Watch the excerpts to check your answer.

1 "[Genealogy] brings history alive."	○	○	"I have three sons, so I see how they fight."
2 "Now, I know there are family feuds."	○	○	"Here's my cousin Gwyneth Paltrow. She has no idea I exist, but we are officially cousins."
3 "So that's 75 million people connected by blood or marriage."	○	○	"I found out I'm connected to Albert Einstein, so I told my seven-year-old son that, and he was totally engaged."

C Work with a partner. Imagine you are giving a talk on the topics below. How could you use personalization?

the cost of living **climate change** **an endangered animal**

A. J. Jacobs at the Global Family Reunion

2E One big happy family

COMMUNICATE Family tree

A Work in a group of four. You are going to work together to draw a family tree.
Student A: Turn to page 141. **Student B**: Turn to page 142.
Student C: Turn to page 144. **Student D**: Turn to page 146.

B Read out pieces of information and ask each other questions to find how everyone is related to each other. Complete the family tree on page 147.

Alice is Steve's wife.

OK. Do they have any children?

Yes, they have a daughter called ...

Checking information

John is ..., isn't he?
Are you saying that they're ....?
So you said that ... ?
Let me just check something, did you say ...?

WRITING An invitation

You are organizing a reunion for your family. Decide when, where, and how long it's going to be. Write a group email to your family members telling them the details.

Hi everyone!

I have great news! I am currently organizing a family reunion, and you're all invited! It's going to take place next July 22–23 during the summer break. It's only going to be two days, but you can stay longer if you like. It's going to be at ...

A family portrait, Idaho, United States

3 Global Stories

“It's often said that you can tell a lot about a person by looking at what's on their bookshelves.”

Ann Morgan
Writer, TED speaker

UNIT GOALS

In this unit, you will ...

- talk about popular books.
- read reviews of several books from around the world.
- watch a TED Talk about an unusual reading goal.

WARM UP

▶ **3.1** Watch part of Ann Morgan's TED Talk. Answer the questions with a partner.

1 Do you agree with the quote above?

2 What do your bookshelves say about you?

The Abbey Library of Saint Gallen, Switzerland, is one of the oldest libraries in the world.

3A Our love of books

VOCABULARY Genres of fiction

A 3.2 Match each genre of fiction to its definition. Listen and check your answers.

1 A fairy tale	is based on characters from a book, movie, or TV show.
2 A horror story	creates fear in the reader.
3 Fan fiction	often includes magical creatures and is usually for children.

4 A graphic novel	has a fictional story and is set in the past.
5 Historical fiction	is drawn like a comic strip.
6 A fantasy story	is usually set in an imaginary, magical world.

7 A romance novel	is an exciting fictional story that is often about crime.
8 A thriller	tells a love story.
9 A sci-fi (science-fiction) story	takes place in the future, often in space.

B Work with a partner. Which genres do you enjoy? Can you think of an example of a book for each one?

C Look at these elements of a story. Then briefly describe one book you have read to your partner.

Characters: who the story is about

Setting: where and when the story takes place

Plot: what happens in the story

Theme: the central idea of the story

LISTENING Interview with an author

A ▶ 3.3 Madeleine Thien is an author. Watch and circle **T** for true or **F** for false.

1. As a child, Thien knew she wanted to be an author. **T** **F**
2. Thien's first book was a collection of short stories. **T** **F**
3. Thien has published three books in total. **T** **F**

Taking notes while listening
When you listen and take notes at the same time, don't write down everything you hear. Be selective and write down only the key words and phrases.

Madeleine Thien

B ▶ 3.3 Watch and complete the chart about the story she describes.

Setting	Characters	Story

C **CRITICAL THINKING**

Reflecting Do you think you'd enjoy this book? Why or why not? Discuss with a partner.

SPEAKING Talking about books

A ▶ 3.4 What's the book about?

A: What are you reading?

B: Oh, it's a book called *And Then There Were None*. Do you know it?

A: No, I don't think so. What kind of book is it? A horror story? — fantasy story / fairy tale

B: No, it's a mystery. It's about a group of people who are stuck on an island together. — It's a story about / It tells the story of

A: It sounds cool. Is it any good? — worth reading / interesting

B: Yeah, I can't put it down.

A: Wow! Can I borrow it when you've finished? — you're done / you've read it

B: Sure. I think you'll like it.

B Practice the conversation with a partner. Practice again using the words on the right.

C Work with a partner. What's your favorite book? Explain what it's about.

My favorite book is *Hyperion* by Dan Simmons. It's a science fiction story about six unique characters who visit the planet Hyperion.

3B What's it about?

LANGUAGE FOCUS Describing stories

A 3.5 Read the information. Which of these books do you know?

B 3.6 Listen to two people talk about one of the books. Complete the sentences.

The Lion, the Witch, and the Wardrobe is a [1]__________ novel about four [2]__________ who live in an old house. They go through a magical wardrobe and visit a place called Narnia. Narnia is a place where [3]__________ can talk.

C 3.7 Watch and study the language in the chart.

Adding details to people, things, and places

People
And Then There Were None is about a group of people who are stuck on an island.
One of the characters is a young man who is rich and handsome.

Things
The Da Vinci Code is a mystery novel that has sold millions of copies worldwide.
A Tale of Two Cities is a piece of historical fiction that is set in London and Paris.

Places
Narnia is a magical place where animals can talk.

For more information on **relative clauses**, see Grammar Summary 3 on page 155.

D Match the two parts of each sentence.

1 *The Hobbit* is a fantasy book	○	○	where two adventurers meet a mysterious queen.
2 *The Da Vinci* Code is about two people	○	○	who studies magic at school.
3 The Harry Potter books are stories	○	○	who investigate a murder in Paris.
4 Harry Potter is a wizard	○	○	that takes place in Middle Earth.
5 *She* is set in a lost African kingdom	○	○	that are popular with kids and adults.

E ▶ **3.8** Find and correct three mistakes. Listen and check your answers.

The Alchemist, by Brazilian novelist Paulo Coelho, is a story about a shepherd boy where travels from Spain to Morocco. He eventually goes to a place in Egypt, looking for treasure that might be buried there. Along the way, he meets people who teaches him many life lessons. It's a story who is both charming and dramatic. I would recommend this book to anyone who wants to read a nice story about becoming who you want to be.

F Complete the sentences with your own ideas. Then compare with a partner.

1 I like stories that ______________________.

2 I like authors who ______________________.

3 I don't enjoy books that ______________________.

4 My favorite book has a character who ______________________.

SPEAKING Can you guess?

A Work alone. Think of a famous book or story. Write three sentences to describe the book in the table below.

	A famous book or story
1	
2	
3	

B Work with a partner. Take turns reading out one of your sentences. After each sentence, try to guess the name of the book.

This is a very famous novel which is set in Russia.

Sorry, I don't know. Give me another clue.

It's about a man who commits a horrible crime.

3C Top picks

PRE-READING Skimming

Skim the text. Why did Ann Morgan like each book?

▶ 3.9 Writer and blogger Ann Morgan loves to share her passion for books. Here are three books she highly recommends.

Lake Como by Srdjan Valjarević

This very funny book follows a Serbian writer named Frank who receives a scholarship[1] and moves to Italy to write. But he doesn't do any work. Instead, he spends his days chatting, watching TV, and sleeping. Frank doesn't write his book, but the connections he makes with the local people take on more importance. The book is about those connections, as well as the meaning of culture and **identity**.

Ann Morgan found it "a great read" and says it "has that rare gift of revealing how people can grow and learn from one another."

Crowfall by Shanta Gokhale

Crowfall is a big, **ambitious** book. The story follows a group of characters who are just starting their careers in Mumbai, India—three painters, a musician, a journalist, and a teacher. The book highlights some **revealing** things about art and music, but is mainly about loss. Throughout the story, there are several deaths that occur, and a loved one goes missing.

Morgan called this book "a **marvelous** read," and especially loved the author's clear, powerful language.

The Blue Sky by Galsan Tschinag

The Blue Sky is a coming-of-age story[2] about a young boy named Dshurukuwaa who lives in Mongolia's Altai Mountains. It's a world that is changing. All around Dshurukuwaa, the traditions of his ancestors are crumbling under the pressures of modern life. In the novel, we get a fascinating **glimpse** into a way of living that is disappearing quickly.

This was one of Morgan's favorite books. She wrote in her blog that it was "impossible not to feel connected to and invested in this world."

[1] **scholarship:** *n.* a sum of money meant to support a student's education

[2] **coming-of-age story:** *n.* a story that focuses on a character's growth from youth to adulthood

UNDERSTANDING DETAILS

A What is the plot of each story? Match the two parts of each sentence.

1 *Lake Como* is about	○	○	a group of people and the losses some of them experience.
2 *Crowfall* is about	○	○	a boy and the changes that are happening in his culture.
3 *The Blue Sky* is about	○	○	a writer who makes meaningful connections with people.

B Complete the chart.

Title	Setting	Characters	Theme
Lake Como			
Crowfall			
The Blue Sky			

MAKING INFERENCES

Which comment do you think probably belongs to each book? Match.

1 *Lake Como*	○	○	"It's sad that customs from the past are no longer practiced today."
2 *Crowfall*	○	○	"It made me think a lot about my grandmother. She died last year."
3 *The Blue Sky*	○	○	"I couldn't put it down I was laughing so hard."

BUILDING VOCABULARY

A Match each word in **blue** from the passage to its definition.

1 **identity**	○	○	giving information
2 **ambitious**	○	○	extremely good
3 **revealing**	○	○	the beliefs and qualities of a person
4 **glimpse**	○	○	wanting to be successful
5 **marvelous**	○	○	a quick look

B **CRITICAL THINKING**

Evaluating Which book would you prefer to read? Why? Discuss with a partner.

3D My year reading a book from every country

TEDTALKS

ANN MORGAN made an **alarming** discovery several years ago when she looked at her bookshelves and saw how **narrow** her reading focus was. Her idea worth spreading is that stories from other countries and cultures have **extraordinary** power to introduce new values and ideas, and to show us our own **blind spots**.

PREVIEWING

Read the paragraph above. Match each **bold** word to its meaning. You will hear these words in the TED Talk.

1 limited: ________________

2 frightening: ________________

3 impressive; remarkable: ________________

4 things you aren't aware of: ________________

VIEWING

A ▶ 3.10 Watch Part 1 of the TED Talk. Answer the questions.

1 What did Morgan discover about her bookshelf?

a Most of the books she owned were the same genre.

b Most of her books were by American or British authors.

c Most of the books she owned were set in England.

2 What goal did Morgan set for herself?

a She would read one book from a different country every year.

b She would read a book from every country in a year.

c She would start to translate books from other countries.

B ▶ 3.11 Watch Part 2 of the TED Talk. Number the events in the order they happened from 1 to 5.

_______ Strangers began to offer suggestions.

_______ Morgan asked for book suggestions.

_______ Friends and family began to offer suggestions.

___1___ Morgan registered her blog.

_______ Morgan received two books from someone in Malaysia.

C ▶ 3.11 Watch Part 2 of the TED Talk again. What surprised Morgan about the response to her project? Discuss with a partner.

D ▶ **3.12** Watch Part 3 of the TED Talk. What did Morgan learn from her experience? Check [✓] the statements that she would agree with.

- ☐ You see the world in a different way.
- ☐ The countries that you read about begin to feel more real.
- ☐ You can get a rounded picture of a country by reading a book.
- ☐ Books have the power to connect people.

E **CRITICAL THINKING**

Applying Morgan's project opened her eyes to new ideas and experiences. What other projects could someone do to achieve the same goal?

VOCABULARY IN CONTEXT

▶ **3.13** Watch the excerpts from the TED Talk. Choose the correct meaning of the words.

PRESENTATION SKILLS Closing a presentation

One way to close a presentation is to ask the audience to join you in supporting or acting on something. Here are other ways to close a presentation.

Summarize your main points.	*Show a powerful visual.*
Give an inspiring quote.	*Circle back to the opener.*
Add a personal story.	*Describe your hope for the future.*

A ▶ **3.14** Watch part of Morgan's TED Talk. How does she end her presentation?

a She shows a powerful visual.

b She gives a quote from an author.

c She talks about her hopes for the future.

B ▶ **3.15** Now watch TED speaker Munir Virani. Check [✓] the ways he closes his presentation.

- ☐ He shows powerful visuals.
- ☐ He gives a call to action.
- ☐ He shares a personal story.
- ☐ He asks the audience a question.

C Work in a group. Whose closing do you think is more effective—Virani's or Morgan's? Why?

3E A good read

COMMUNICATE A book recommendation

A Work in a group. Brainstorm a list of books from your country. Include books from a variety of genres, such as novels, autobiographies, children's stories, and fiction.

B Imagine that Ann Morgan asked you for a suggestion on a book to read from your country. Agree on one book and list two reasons why it's a good choice.

Book title:

Author: Genre:

What it's about:

Reason 1:

Reason 2:

In your opinion, which book best represents our country?

I think we should suggest ...

Asking for opinions
Which do you think ...? *In your opinion, what's ...?* *What do you feel is ...?*

C Take turns presenting your book suggestions. Answer any questions from the class.

WRITING Book review

A Write a short review about a book you read. Include the title, author, and information about the setting, characters, and plot.

A strange but interesting story ★★★★

I recently read *The Vegetarian* by Korean writer Han Kang. The story takes place in South Korea. The main characters are Yeong-hye and her husband, Mr. Cheong. It's about a wife who doesn't want to follow society's rules. After she has a frightening dream, she decides to become a vegetarian.

B Work in a group. Read each other's reviews. In your opinion, which book sounds the most interesting? Why?

Presentation 1

MODEL PRESENTATION

A Complete the transcript of the presentation using the words in the box.

cousin	endangered	facing	going to	help
reptile	that	traveling	where	work

I'd like to talk to you about an amazing [1] __________ that really needs our help—the sea turtle. Last month, I went diving off the coast of Mozambique in Africa with my [2] __________, Maria. I saw so many amazing things, but the animal [3] __________ I remember more than any others was this beautiful loggerhead sea turtle. My dive instructor told me how lucky I was. He said that sea turtles were [4] __________ and seeing one wasn't so common any more. I later found out that many turtles are killed by humans for their eggs, meat, skin, and shells. The turtles' habitats and the coastal areas [5] __________ they lay their eggs are also under threat. So, how can you [6] __________? Well, firstly, when you're [7] __________, be careful what you buy. Ask questions if you think a souvenir might be made from a turtle shell. Secondly, support a turtle charity. There are many organizations that [8] __________ to help save sea turtles. I'm now a member of a sea turtle charity and next month I'm [9] __________ take part in a fundraising event. Finally, you can spread the word. Tell other people about these animals and the dangers they are [10] __________.

Thank you so much.

B ▶ **P.1** Watch the presentation and check your answers.

C ▶ **P.1** Review the list of presentation skills from Units 1–3 below. Which does the speaker use? Check [✓] each skill used as you watch again.

The speaker …

- ☐ uses questions to signpost
- ☐ personalizes the presentation
- ☐ closes the presentation effectively

D Look at the notes the speaker made before her presentation. Did she forget to say anything?

- Introduction: amazing reptile / sea turtle
- Trip to Mozambique / diving
- Dive instructor / lucky / endangered
- Turtles killed for eggs/meat, etc. / habitat threatened
- How can you help?
- Careful what you buy and eat when abroad
- Support a charity / spread the word

YOUR TURN

A You are going to plan and give a short presentation to a partner introducing an endangered animal. Use the notes above for ideas and research any other information. Make notes on a card or a small piece of paper.

B Look at the useful phrases in the box below. Think about which ones you will need in your presentation.

Useful phrases

Introducing your topic:	*I'd like to (tell you/talk to you) about ...*
Types of animals:	*amphibians, birds, fish, insects, mammals, reptiles*
Describing conservation status:	*threatened, vulnerable, (critically) endangered, extinct*
Signposting questions:	*Why do they need our help? / How can you help?*
Ending:	*Thank you so much (for listening).* *Thanks for listening.*

C Work with a partner. Take turns giving your presentation using your notes. Use some of the presentation skills from Units 1–3. As you listen, check [✓] each skill your partner uses.

The speaker ...

- ☐ uses questions to signpost
- ☐ personalizes the presentation
- ☐ closes the presentation effectively

D Give your partner some feedback on their talk. Include two things you liked, and one thing he or she can improve.

> Well done! You spoke really clearly and I loved the way you personalized the presentation. Next time, try to make more eye contact with your audience.

4 Music

UNIT GOALS

In this unit, you will ...

- talk about how music affects us.
- read about why music makes us feel good.
- watch a TED Talk by a musician who gives unusual concerts.

WARM UP

▶ 4.1 Watch part of Daria van den Bercken's TED Talk. Answer the questions with a partner.

1 What kind of music does van den Bercken play?
2 Do you like this kind of music?

Fans reach out to touch their music idol.

4A Feel the music

VOCABULARY Music

A ▶ 4.2 Listen and number the musical genres from 1 to 6 in the order you hear them.

_____ classical
_____ country
_____ electronic
_____ easy listening
_____ heavy metal
_____ hip-hop

B Complete the chart with words from the box.

energized	loud	soothing	relaxed	soft	sleepy

Words to describe music		How music makes you feel	
dark	_____	nostalgic	_____
upbeat	_____	melancholic	_____
rhythmic	_____	romantic	_____

C ▶ 4.2 Listen again to the music from **A**. Work with a partner. Describe each piece of music.

The easy listening music is very soft.

Yeah, it makes me feel very relaxed.

LISTENING A traditional singer

Understanding accents
At first, an unfamiliar accent can be difficult to understand. Try to identify the vowel sounds that are different and listen to other examples of the same accent to increase your familiarity with it.

A ▶ 4.3 Iarla Ó Lionáird is a musician who sings in a style called *sean-nós*. Watch the video. Which country does sean-nós singing come from?

B ▶ 4.3 Watch again. Circle **T** for True or **F** for False.

1	Ó Lionáird sings in English.	**T**	**F**
2	Some of his relatives were also singers.	**T**	**F**
3	Ó Lionáird's teacher, Mrs. McSweeney, encouraged him to sing.	**T**	**F**
4	Ó Lionáird released his first solo album in 2014.	**T**	**F**

C **CRITICAL THINKING**

Personalizing What words would you use to describe Ó Lionáird's music? How does the music make you feel? Discuss with a partner

Iarla Ó Lionáird performing live

SPEAKING Talking about music

A ▶ 4.4 What kind of music is the man listening to?

A: What are you listening to?

B: Oh, it's a band called *The National*. Here, listen.

A: Hey, they're pretty good. I've never heard them before.

B: Yeah, they're not so famous, but they've been around a while. They've done a lot of albums. — well-known / popular; made / produced

A: This song's great. I love this kind of melancholic rock.

B: Me too. But they have a few really loud, upbeat songs, too. Here, listen to this one. — some / one or two

A: Wow! I see what you mean. Do you have many of their albums?

B: I have them all. And they have a concert here in July. I can't wait. — gig / show

B Practice the conversation with a partner. Practice again using the words on the right.

C Work with a partner. Tell each other about a band or singer that you like. Explain why.

> I really like Norah Jones. She has some really romantic songs, and she has such a good voice.

> Yeah, me too. I have a few of her albums.

4B Just the right music

LANGUAGE FOCUS Discussing types of music

A ▶ **4.5** Read the information. When should you listen to classical music?

WHAT'S THE BEST MUSIC FOR ...?

STUDYING

Best music: classical or instrumental music
Examples: Mozart's sonatas or Spanish guitar
Why? It makes it easier for you to concentrate and take in new information.

GETTING TO SLEEP

Best music: soft classical music
Examples: the works of Handel and Bach
Why? It slows down brainwaves and helps you relax.

EXERCISING

Best music: electronic, hip-hop, or pop songs
Examples: Lady Gaga's *Applause*
Why? It has a fast and regular rhythm.

DRIVING

Best music: pop songs with a gentle tempo
Examples: Justin Timberlake's *Cry Me a River*
Why? The rhythm matches your heartbeat and keeps you calm so you drive carefully.

B ▶ **4.6** Listen to a music expert talk about the best music to listen to while studying. Circle the correct words to complete the recommendations.

1 Listen to songs (**with** / **without**) words.

2 Listen to (**the radio** / **your favorite album**).

C ▶ **4.7** Watch and study the language in the chart.

Talking about quantity

Things you can count	*Things you cannot count*
I like this song. I like these songs.	I like this music.
There were too many people.	There was too much noise.
Do you have many songs on your phone? I have a lot of pop songs. I don't have many country songs.	Do you have much music on your phone? I have a lot of pop music. I don't have much country music.
How many people were at the concert? There were a lot / many. There were only a few.	How much traffic was there? There was a lot. There was only a little.

For more information on **countable and uncountable nouns**, see Grammar Extension 4 on page 156.

D Circle the correct words.

1 **A:** Do you like (**this music / these music**)?
  B: I do. Do you know where I can download some (**song / songs**)?

2 **A:** Did it take (**many / much**) time to download that new song?
  B: Yeah. I think too (**many / much**) people were trying to download it at once.

3 **A:** (**Were / Was**) there a big crowd at the concert?
  B: Not really. There were only a (**few / little**) people.

E Correct the mistake in each sentence.

1 I love this band but they don't do many live concert these days.

2 The performer stopped because there was too many noise coming from the crowd.

3 I was amazed by how few equipment the band had on stage.

4 After the band finished their last song, there were a lot of applause.

F ▶ 4.8 Complete the information. Circle the correct words. Listen and check your answers.

If you're a student who's struggling with too [1](**many / much**) exams, a [2](**few / little**) classical music might just help. According to [3](**many / much**) different academic studies, classical music has [4](**many / much**) benefits for your brain and body that can make a difference at exam time. It's been shown that listening to classical music has an effect on how [5](**many / much**) new information you can learn. And if you're stressed or not getting [6](**many / much**) sleep, classical music can help, too. It can help you relax, and is also said to reduce blood pressure.

SPEAKING Musical preferences

A Interview your partner. Take notes.

What's the best music for ...?	Music
getting to sleep	
when you feel sad	
a party	
studying late at night	
a long-distance drive	
a romantic dinner	

What do you think is the best music for relaxing?

I think jazz is the best. It's very soothing.

B Work in a group. Share the most interesting information you heard.

A woman plays the violin during an orchestral performance.

4C Music and the brain

PRE-READING Previewing

4.9 Listen to part of Johannes Brahms' Hungarian Dance No. 5. How does it make you feel? Discuss with a partner.

4.10

1 One day several years ago, Valorie Salimpoor took a drive that changed her life. Salimpoor, a neuroscience[1] graduate, was struggling to decide on her career path. She felt that a drive might help clear her head. When she **turned on** the car radio, a piece of violin music came on: Brahms' Hungarian Dance No. 5. "Something just happened," she recalls. "I just felt this rush of emotion ... It was so intense." She stopped the car so she could focus on the music. She wondered why it had such a powerful **effect** on her.

2 Salimpoor found a job working as a neuroscientist. Her **research** involved scanning people's brain activity as they listened to music. She discovered that when people listen to music they like, their brains flood with dopamine—a **chemical** linked with pleasure and motivation. In one experiment, people listened to the first 30 seconds of unfamiliar songs. The listeners were then given the option of buying the full songs, using their own money. By analyzing dopamine-related areas of the participants' brains, Salimpoor was able to successfully predict which songs the people would choose to buy; she could tell what they liked and what they didn't based on brain activity.

3 But why might one person like a song while another person doesn't? Salimpoor says it all depends on past musical experiences. "Eastern, Western, jazz, heavy metal, pop—all of these have different rules they follow," she says. These rules are recorded as patterns, or templates, in the brain. If the new music has a familiar template, your brain releases dopamine and **registers** a feeling of pleasure. This might explain why most people have a preference for a certain type of music.

4 There are questions Salimpoor is still trying to answer: How does our brain make musical templates? Why do people with similar backgrounds have different preferences? Her research, though, has given her a new way to think about her experience years ago. "That day," she says, "it all seemed like such a big mystery." Now when she hears a piece of music she likes, she has a better understanding of what's happening inside her brain.

[1] **neuroscience:** *n.* the study of the brain and nervous system

UNDERSTANDING GIST

Read the passage. Which two questions does the passage discuss?

a Why does music affect our emotions?

b What is the happiest music to listen to?

c When did our brains first hear music?

d Why do different people like different kinds of music?

UNDERSTANDING DETAILS

Circle the best answer for each question.

1 Why was Hungarian Dance No. 5 special for Salimpoor?

- **a** It brought back a very happy memory.
- **b** It had a strong effect on her career.
- **c** It made her think of a favorite piece of music.

2 What is the main idea of Paragraph 2?

- **a** An experiment showed that classical music usually makes people happy.
- **b** Researchers found a link between music and chemical activity in the brain.
- **c** According to a study, certain types of music can slow down brain activity.

3 What are the "templates" referred to in Paragraph 3?

- **a** special tools that are used in brain scan experiments
- **b** types of music that have a very strong emotional impact
- **c** patterns in the brain that relate to certain types of music

4 The following sentence would be best placed at the end of which paragraph?

Right then, she decided her future career.

a Paragraph 1 **b** Paragraph 2 **c** Paragraph 3

5 What does "mystery" in Paragraph 4 refer to?

- **a** where memory templates are stored in the brain
- **b** which part of the brain produces the most dopamine
- **c** what happens in our brains when we listen to music

BUILDING VOCABULARY

A Complete each sentence using the correct form of the words in **blue** from the passage.

1 A scientist usually has to do a lot of ____________ as part of their job.

2 ____________ released by our brains can effect our emotions.

3 The earthquake ____________ 7.2 on the Richter scale.

4 You can ____________ your TV with a remote control.

5 Certain songs can have an emotional ____________ on people.

B **CRITICAL THINKING**

Applying What kinds of music have the greatest effect on you? Why do you think those types of music are special? Discuss with a partner.

4D Why I take the piano on the road ... and in the air

TEDTALKS

A few years ago, **DARIA VAN DEN BERCKEN** discovered George Handel's keyboard music. When she started to play it, she was in complete **awe**. What she experienced that day set her on a journey to share the beauty of music with others. Her idea worth spreading is that we should try to enjoy music the way a child does—full of **wonder** and with pure, **unprejudiced** amazement.

PREVIEWING

A Read the paragraph above. Circle the correct option for each sentence below. You will hear these words in the TED Talk.

1 If you are **in awe of** something, you (**admire**/**cannot appreciate**) it.

2 You are likely to be full of **wonder** (**on a beautiful mountain**/**in a dark room**).

3 When you are **unprejudiced**, you have (**an open**/**a closed**) mind about something.

B ▶ 4.11 Watch van den Bercken play two pieces of music. How do you think she describes each piece? Circle your ideas.

Piece 1: a melancholic **b** relaxing **Piece 2: a** energetic **b** romantic

VIEWING

A ▶ 4.12 Watch Part 1 of the TED Talk. Circle the correct answers.

1 Why was van den Bercken surprised by the music she found on the Internet?

a She didn't know Handel wrote keyboard music. **b** It was extremely difficult to play.

2 Why was she "in awe" of the music?

a because it was so difficult to play **b** because it changed from sad to energetic

B ▶ 4.13 Watch Part 2 of the TED Talk. Who does van den Bercken describe when she makes these claims? Check [✓] the correct column.

	7- and 8-year-olds	11- and 12-year-olds
1 They're willing to listen to classical music.		
2 It's hard to get them to listen to classical music.		
3 The opinions of others matter to them.		
4 They listen to music without prejudice.		

C CRITICAL THINKING

Reflecting How have your musical tastes changed since you were a child? Discuss with a partner.

VOCABULARY IN CONTEXT

▶ 4.14 Watch the excerpts from the TED Talk. Choose the correct meaning of the words.

PRESENTATION SKILLS Providing background information

> During a presentation, it's often useful to include some information about your own background. This can help the audience understand why you're interested in the topic you're talking about.

A ▶ 4.15 Watch the excerpt. What background information does van den Bercken provide?

a who first got her interested in learning the piano

b how she learned something new about a composer

c the first time she heard someone play Handel's music

B ▶ 4.16 Now watch two other TED speakers. Match the speakers to the background information they give. One is extra.

1 A. J. Jacobs	○	○	**a** a meeting with a famous person
2 Ann Morgan	○	○	**b** an email that inspired them
		○	**c** what they learned about themselves

C Work in a group. Think of something you are passionate about. Now imagine you are going to give a presentation about it. What background information about yourself would you provide?

“I fell in love with the music and I wanted to share it with as many people as possible.”

4E Musical choices

COMMUNICATE Desert island discs

A Imagine you are going to spend a year alone on a desert island. You can choose four songs to take with you and listen to while you're there. Write your list in the space below.

1	______________________	3	______________________
2	______________________	4	______________________

B Look at the questions below and prepare to answer them for each song on your list. Research any information you don't know.

Who wrote the song?	**What words would you use to describe the song?**
When was it written?	**Why is it important to you?**

C Work with a partner. Use the questions above to interview each other. Ask for extra information.

D Listen to each other's songs. Tell your partner your opinion.

Describing music
It makes me feel … *It sounds …* *It reminds me of …* *When I listen to it, I …*

WRITING A favorite song

Think of one more of your favorite songs. Explain how it makes you feel and why you like it. Does it have any special significance?

One of my favorite songs is *Wake Up* by Arcade Fire. I like it because it's a really powerful and energetic song, and it makes me feel happy. It reminds me of my time at university.

A man stands on a desert island in the Seychelles.

5 Good Design

“ Trust me. One hundred percent of people care about flags. ”

Roman Mars
Digital storyteller, TED speaker

UNIT GOALS

In this unit, you will ...

- talk about design.
- read about the importance of city flags.
- watch a TED Talk about good flag design.

WARM UP

▶ **5.1** Watch part of Roman Mars's TED Talk. Answer the questions with a partner.

1 Describe a flag you know well.

2 Do you think it has a good design? Why or why not?

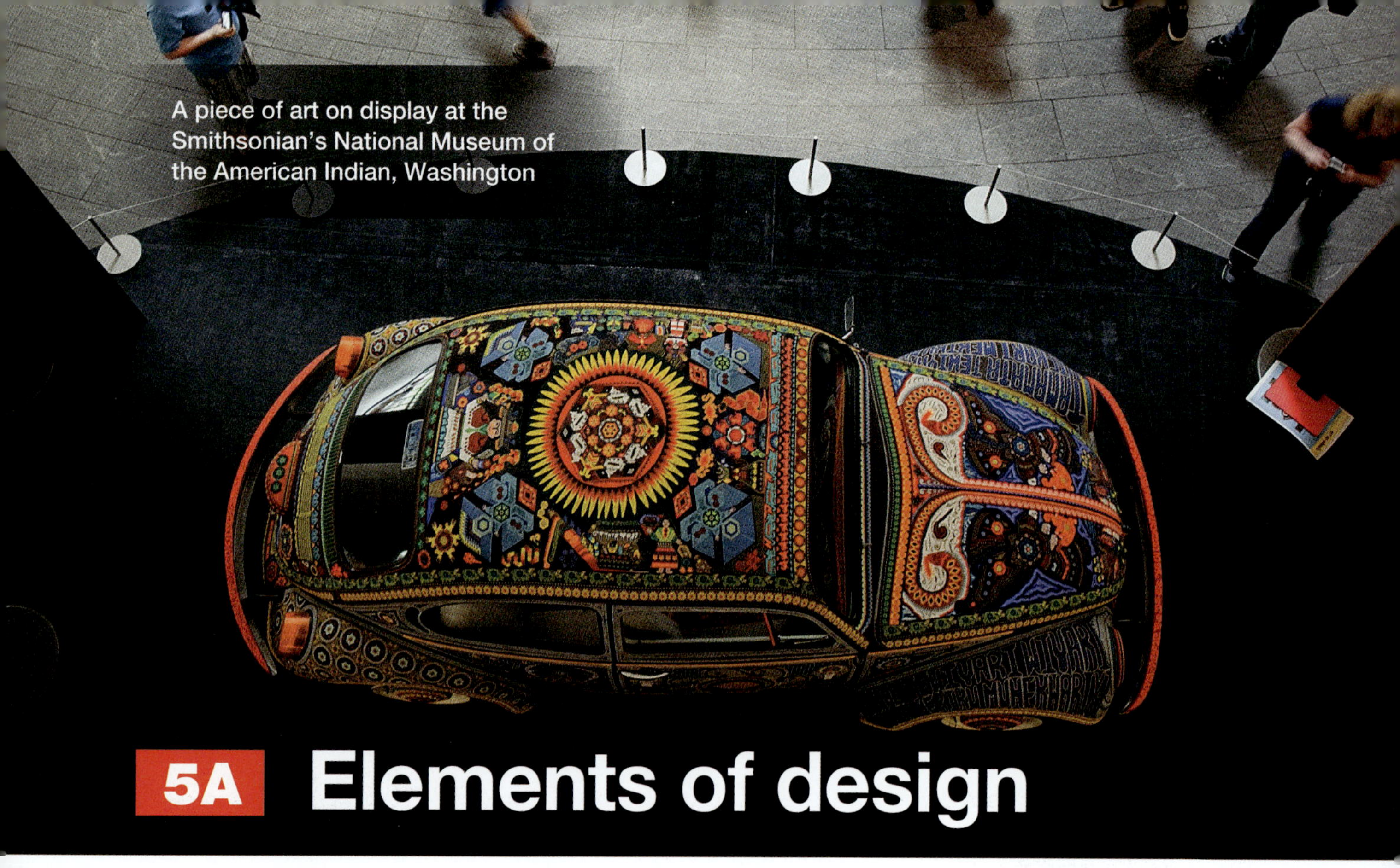

A piece of art on display at the Smithsonian's National Museum of the American Indian, Washington

5A Elements of design

VOCABULARY Design elements

A These words can be used to describe visual designs, including art. ~~Cross out~~ the word that does not belong in each category.

1 colors	bright	short	pale	vibrant	________
2 lines	straight	happy	curved	thick	________
3 shape	pale	round	triangular	square	________
4 size	orange	tiny	large	huge	________
5 texture	silky	empty	rough	smooth	________
6 contrast	subtle	sharp	tall	dramatic	________

B Work with a partner. Add one more word to each category.

C Work with a partner. Which of the words in **A** could be used to describe the art in the picture above?

D Do you like the art in the picture above? Why or why not? Discuss with a partner.

I like it. The colors are really vibrant.

Me too. I like the bright colors and the curved lines.

LISTENING A designer's advice

Identifying changes in topic
There are certain phrases in English that are used to signify a change in topic.

In regard to ...   *As far as ... is concerned*   *Regarding ...*

A ▶ 5.2 Sarah Lafferty is an interior designer. Watch and complete the quote she gives.

"Have nothing in your houses that you do not know to be ________ or believe to be ________."

William Morris, designer

B ▶ 5.2 Watch again. Circle the correct option to complete the sentences.

1 Lafferty's parents were (**architects**/**interior designers**).

2 Lafferty studied (**interior**/**textile**) design at university.

3 Lafferty wants the houses she designs to reflect her (**clients'**/**own**) tastes.

Sarah Lafferty

C **CRITICAL THINKING**

Applying Look again at the quote by William Morris. If you apply this idea to your own home, what would you need to change? Discuss with a partner.

SPEAKING Talking about design

A ▶ 5.3 Do you think the people will buy the sofa?

A: What do you think of this one?

B: This one? Don't you think the colors are a bit too bright? — strong / vibrant

A: No, I love the colors. And the shape is perfect for our living room. — ideal / just right

B: Yeah, but I don't think it will go with the rest of our furniture. — match / look good with

A: Why not?

B: All our other furniture is brown. This has yellow and pink stripes.

A: Our walls are yellow.

B: Yeah, but it's a very pale yellow. Can we look at something else, please? — light / soft

B Practice the conversation with a partner. Practice again using the words on the right.

C Work with a partner. Turn to page 147. What do you like and dislike about each piece of furniture?

I like the shape and the colors.

I agree. But I think they're too bright.

5B Signs of the times

LANGUAGE FOCUS Discussing elements of design

A ▶ 5.4 Read the information. What were coats of arms originally for?

COATS OF ARMS

were originally used to establish identity in battle. They later evolved to show family descent, property ownership, and profession. Each coat of arms is unique but they have many of the same elements.

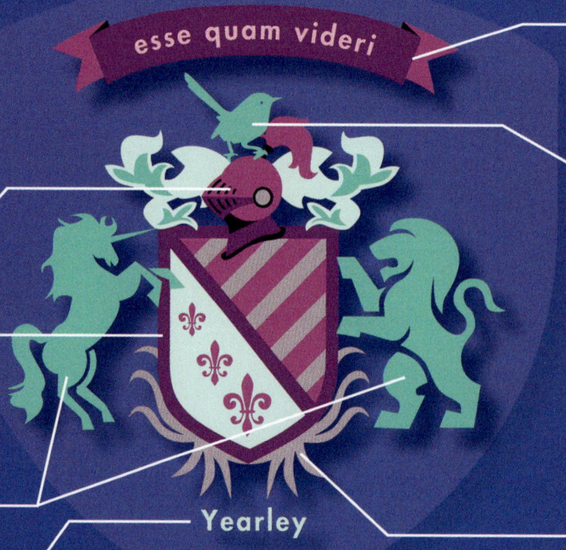

B ▶ 5.5 Listen to an expert explain the parts of a coat of arms. Circle the correct words.

1 (**All** / **Not all**) coats of arms have a motto.

2 Sometimes the motto is (**below** / **on**) the shield.

3 The two supporters are (**always** / **usually**) animals.

4 The shape of the shield (**has** / **has no**) meaning.

C ▶ 5.6 Watch and study the language in the chart.

Talking about place and position	
There's a horn on the unicorn's head. Some shields are in the shape of a square.	There's a unicorn on the left / on the right. There's a lion to the left of / to the right of the shield.
There's a banner at the top. The family name is at the bottom.	The motto is above the crest. The family name is below the shield.
The shield is in front of the mantle. The mantle is behind the shield. There's a border around the shield.	Three gray flowers are in / inside the blue square. The shield is in the center / in the middle.

For more information on **prepositions of place**, see Grammar Extension 5 on page 156.

D Look at the coat of arms on page 58. Complete the sentences.

1 The motto is ______on______ the banner.

2 The banner and motto are ____________ the shield.

3 There is a lion to the ____________ of the shield.

4 There are symbols and stripes ____________ the shield.

5 ____________ the shield is a thick border.

6 The crest is ____________ the banner.

E Find and correct the mistake in each description.

1 A "No Parking" sign in the United States is a black *P* on a white circle. There is a red border across the circle with a slash through the *P*.

2 A stop sign in Brazil is at the shape of an octagon. It is red and has the word *Pare* (Portuguese for *stop*) written on it.

3 A "Kangaroo Crossing" sign in Australia is a yellow diamond-shaped sign with a black image of a kangaroo below it.

F ▶ 5.7 Complete the information. Circle the correct words. Listen and check your answers.

Most countries in Europe use similar road signs. This makes it easy for visitors to understand them. For example, a yield sign is [1](**in** / **on**) the shape of an inverted triangle. It's white or yellow and has a red border [2](**across** / **around**) it. A traffic light sign is similar, but the triangle is not inverted—the wide part is at the [3](**middle** / **bottom**). There are three circles [4](**inside** / **outside**) the triangle. The one [5](**at** / **in**) the top is red. The one [6](**in** / **of**) the middle is yellow, and the bottom one is green, just like a traffic light. There are no words [7](**on** / **at**) the sign.

A traffic light sign

SPEAKING Designing a coat of arms

A You are going to design your own personal coat of arms. Look back at the coat of arms on page 58. Decide on a motto and the different design elements. Draw your design, but don't show it to anyone.

B Work in a group. Describe your coat of arms. Your group members will try to draw it.

> There are two supporters. The one on the left is a dolphin. The one on the right is a whale.

> Okay. What pattern is on the shield?

C Show your coat of arms to your group. Whose drawing is the closest to your original?

The Chicago flag can be seen all around the city.

5C Symbol of a city

PRE-READING Previewing

Look at the photo and read the third paragraph of the passage. What do the three parts of Chicago's flag represent?

1 the white areas: ____________ **2** the stripes: ____________ **3** the stars: ____________

▶ 5.8

1 Many cities in the United States have flags, but few are as loved as Chicago's. It can be seen all over the city—from its street corners to its skyscrapers. "Today," says Whet Moser from *Chicago* magazine, "I went to get a haircut. When I sat down in the barber's chair, there was a Chicago flag on the box that the barber kept all his **tools** in. In the mirror, there was a Chicago flag on the wall behind me. When I left, a guy passed me who had a Chicago flag on his backpack." There is even a website called ChicagoFlagTattoos.com. It features interviews with and photos of people who love the flag so much that they want it permanently drawn on their bodies.

2 The flag is also a **distinct** symbol of Chicago pride. As flag expert Ted Kaye says, "When a police officer or a firefighter dies in Chicago, often it's not the flag of the United States on his casket.[1] It can be the flag of the city of Chicago. That's how deeply the flag has gotten into the civic[2] imagery of Chicago."

3 Like any good flag, the Chicago flag's design is simple and its **symbolism** is clear. The white areas represent three Chicago neighborhoods. The stripes represent the river and the lake. The stars represent important events in Chicago's history. Its simple but **bold** design is rated highly by flag experts and is probably also the reason it has become so **popular**.

4 Roman Mars moved to Chicago in 2005, and he too fell in love with the flag. Mars is the host and creator of *99% Invisible*—a popular radio show about design and architecture. He's sure that the love for the flag is not just because people love Chicago. In Mars's own words, "I also think that people love Chicago more because the flag is so cool."

[1] **casket:** *n.* a box in which a dead person is buried

[2] **civic:** *adj.* related to a particular community

UNDERSTANDING MAIN IDEAS

Read the passage. Circle the main idea.

a The flag of Chicago is important to the identity of the city and its people.

b The flag of Chicago is a best-selling souvenir for tourists.

c The flag of Chicago became famous after being featured on a radio show.

UNDERSTANDING SUPPORTING QUOTES

Match each person to the statement that supports their quote.

1 Whet Moser ○		○ The Chicago flag is a symbol of pride for people in the city.
2 Ted Kaye ○		○ People like Chicago more because it has a great flag.
3 Roman Mars ○		○ You can see the Chicago flag all around the city.

UNDERSTANDING DETAILS

Circle **T** for True, **F** for False, or **NG** for Not Given.

1 Chicago is one of few cities in the United States that has a flag.	**T**	**F**	**NG**
2 Whet Moser has a Chicago flag tattoo.	**T**	**F**	**NG**
3 The Chicago flag can be seen during some people's funerals.	**T**	**F**	**NG**
4 Experts in flag design like the Chicago flag.	**T**	**F**	**NG**
5 Roman Mars has lived in Chicago all his life.	**T**	**F**	**NG**

BUILDING VOCABULARY

A Circle the correct option to complete each sentence.

1 **Symbolism** refers to what something ______.
  a looks like **b** means or represents

2 A flag with a **bold** design is ______ to see or notice.
  a easy **b** difficult

3 If something is **popular**, many people ______ it.
  a like **b** trust

4 An example of a barber's **tool** is ______.
  a a customer **b** a pair of scissors

5 A design that is **distinct** is ______ others.
  a similar to **b** different from

B **CRITICAL THINKING**

Applying What events in your city's history could be represented on a flag? Discuss with a partner.

5D The worst-designed thing you've never noticed

TEDTALKS

ROMAN MARS tells stories about design on the radio. His **mission** is to get people to **engage with** designs they find compelling so that they begin to **pay attention to** all forms of design. He especially loves flags. His idea worth spreading is that a well-designed city flag can be an object of beauty, strengthen civic pride, and have economic benefits.

PREVIEWING

A Read the paragraph above. Circle the correct option for each sentence below. You will hear these words in the TED Talk.

1 A **mission** is something you (**need** / **don't need**) to do.

2 If you **engage with** something, you (**ignore** / **show interest in**) it.

3 When you **pay attention to** something, you (**buy** / **concentrate on**) it.

B Look at these flags of Canada and San Francisco. What do you like about each design?

VIEWING

A ▶ 5.9 Watch Part 1 of the TED Talk. Which flag does Mars prefer? Why? Discuss with a partner.

B Read the following excerpt from Part 1 of the TED Talk. How does the San Francisco flag compare with what you learned about the Chicago flag on page 60? Discuss with a partner.

"So when I moved back to San Francisco in 2008, I researched its flag, because I had never seen it in the previous eight years I lived there."

C ▶ **5.10** Complete the notes below with words from the box. Watch Part 2 of the TED Talk to check your guesses.

bigger	colors	name	enlarge
middle	simple	simplify	writing

Five principles of flag design	To improve San Francisco's flag:
1 *Keep it ________ .*	*Remove the motto.*
2 *Use meaningful symbolism.*	*Remove ________ .*
3 *Use only two to three basic ________ .*	*________ border.*
4 *Do not use ________ of any kind.*	*Make the phoenix (bird) ________ and move to ________ .*
5 *Be distinctive.*	*________ or stylize the phoenix.*

D ▶ **5.11** Watch Part 3 of the TED Talk. Check [✓] the statements that Mars would probably agree with.

☐ City flags can bring people together.

☐ Pocatello has a terrible flag.

☐ A good flag should have a trademark symbol.

E CRITICAL THINKING

Applying To design a great flag, Mars says you should first draw a rectangle of this size so that you can see it from a distance. Draw a flag you know in the space to the right. Based on this, does your flag have a good design?

VOCABULARY IN CONTEXT

▶ **5.12** Watch the excerpts from the TED Talk. Choose the correct meaning of the words.

PRESENTATION SKILLS Numbering key points

Numbering your points in your talk (*one, two, three*, or *first, second, third*, etc.) can help your audience follow along more easily.

A ▶ **5.13** Watch the excerpt. Notice how the points are numbered.

B ▶ **5.14** Now watch excerpts of TED speaker A. J. Jacobs giving four reasons why a world family tree is important. Circle the numbers you hear.

1 One / First **2** Two / Second **3** Three / Third **4** Four / Fourth

C Work in a group. Think of three things you learned in this unit. Then share them using numbers.

I learned three things about flags. First, most cities have them. Second, …

5E Meaningful design

COMMUNICATE A new city flag

A Work in a group. Look at these city flags. Which one do you like the most? Which one do you like the least? Why?

B Work with a partner. You are going to design a new flag for your city. First, write down four or five things that your city is famous for. Think about famous places and historical events.

C Work together to design and sketch your flag. Keep Roman Mars's principles of design in mind.

1. Keep it simple.
2. Use meaningful symbolism.
3. Use only two to three basic colors.
4. Do not use writing of any kind.
5. Be distinctive.

D Draw your flag on a bigger sheet of paper. Then present your flag to the class. Explain what the different parts of your flag represent and any other design choices you made.

Talking about meaning

What is the meaning of ...?	*It means ...*
What does ... represent?	*It represents ...*
What does ... symbolize?	*It symbolizes ...*

WRITING My country's flag

Look back at the sketch you drew of the flag on page 63. Do some research and then write about what the flag means.

> The design of my country's flag is very simple. It uses three colors—green, black, and white. There are three vertical stripes and in the upper left corner there is a ...

6 Inspiration

"The doorbell rang and it was a trick-or-treater dressed as my character. It was so cool."

Jarrett Krosoczka
Author, TED speaker

UNIT GOALS

In this unit, you will ...

- talk about inspirational people.
- read about how someone became an author.
- watch a TED Talk about the events that inspired an author's career.

WARM UP

▶ 6.1 Watch part of Jarrett Krosoczka's TED Talk. Answer the questions with a partner.

1 What kind of books does Krosoczka write?

2 Why did Krosoczka think the trick-or-treater was "so cool"?

A boy and his father launch a model rocket.

6A Inspiring people

VOCABULARY Sources of inspiration

A ▶ 6.2 Complete the sentences with words from the box. Listen and check your answers.

changed	encouraged	gave
showed	supported	was

1 "When I met my best friend Maria, she completely __________ my life."

2 "My biology teacher, Mrs. Chang, __________ me to become a scientist."

3 "My first boss __________ a great role-model for me when I first started work."

4 "My mother __________ me that it's possible to stay positive even in difficult times."

5 "I was lucky that my parents always __________ my career in music."

6 "My grandfather always __________ me great advice when I was young."

B Change two or three of the sentences in **A** to make them true for you.

C Work with a partner. Read your sentences to each other. Ask questions as you listen.

> My older brother was a great role-model for me when I was a child.

> Yeah? In what way?

LISTENING My inspiration

Hedging
It is common for English speakers to use certain words or phrases to indicate uncertainty. Common hedging words include:
probably *possibly* *maybe* *perhaps*

Former NASA astronaut Franklin Chang Díaz

A ▶ **6.3** Franklin Chang Díaz is a former NASA astronaut. Who does he describe as his "number one hero"? Watch and circle the correct answer.

a his science teacher **b** a famous astronaut **c** his father

B ▶ **6.3** Watch again. Circle **T** for True or **F** for False.

1	As an astronaut, Chang Díaz went into space only once.	**T**	**F**
2	Chang Díaz became interested in space when he was a child.	**T**	**F**
3	Chang Díaz's father was a scientist.	**T**	**F**
4	Chang Díaz believes he is an inspiration for others.	**T**	**F**

C **CRITICAL THINKING**

Inferring Chang Díaz says that "Inspiration is in many ways a bit of a chain." What does he mean by this? Discuss with a partner.

SPEAKING Talking about an inspirational person

A ▶ **6.4** What was the music teacher's advice?

A: When did you graduate from university?
B: About three years ago. I kind of miss being a student. — A couple of / Just a few
A: I know what you mean. What did you study? — did you major in / was your major
B: Business administration. What about you?
A: I majored in music.
B: Yeah? Why did you choose that?
A: I had a great music teacher at school. She really inspired me. — was really inspiring / was an inspiration
B: That's cool.
A: Yeah. She always told me to follow my passion in life. It was really great advice. — advised me to / said that I should

B Practice the conversation with a partner. Practice again using the words on the right.

C Think of three inspiring people. Use these examples or think of others. Tell your partner why they inspire you.

a family member **a teacher** **a leader** **an athlete** **a historical figure**

Serena Williams is really inspiring. She's an amazing athlete who never gives up and always wants to improve.

6B Inspiring words

LANGUAGE FOCUS Discussing inspirational people

A ▶ 6.5 Read the information. What else do you know about these people?

THE WORLD'S MOST INSPIRATIONAL PEOPLE

A recent survey identified 50 of the world's most inspiring people. Here are the top 3.

NELSON MANDELA

1918–2013
Former President of South Africa

"Education is the most powerful weapon which you can use to change the world."

MAHATMA GANDHI

1869–1948
Leader of independence movement in India

"You must be the change you wish to see in the world."

STEVE JOBS

1955–2011
Cofounder, chairman, and CEO of Apple, Inc.

"Innovation distinguishes between a leader and a follower."

THESE PEOPLE ALSO MADE THE LIST: Leonardo da Vinci (Italy), Anne Frank (Germany), Frida Kahlo (Mexico), Bob Marley (Jamaica), Coco Chanel (France), Stephen Hawking (England), Martin Luther King Jr. (U.S.).

B ▶ 6.6 Listen to someone talking about two people he admires. Complete the chart.

Who does he admire?	Why does he admire them?
1	
2	

C ▶ 6.7 Watch and study the language in the chart.

Reporting what someone said

"I admire Frida Kahlo."	He said He told me	(that) he admired Frida Kahlo.
"I don't know much about her."	He said He told me	(that) he didn't know much about her.
"Follow your dreams." "Don't be afraid."	He told me to follow my dreams. He told me not to be afraid.	

For more information on **reported speech**, see Grammar Summary 6 on page 156.

D Circle the correct option to complete each sentence.

1 My teacher (**said / told**) me not to interrupt while other people are talking.

2 My father (**said / told**) that he had two jobs when he was a student.

3 Her older brother (**said / told**) her to take her piano lessons more seriously.

4 My coach (**said / told**) me that I was his most promising new player.

5 Our professor always (**said / told**) us that there was no success without failure.

E Rewrite the sentences as reported speech.

1 "Think carefully about your future."	My dad told me ________________.
2 "I want to lead our country someday."	My sister said ________________.
3 "Don't make the same mistake twice."	The teacher told her ________________.
4 "I don't want to stand in your way."	My mother told me ________________.
5 "I don't worry about the little things."	My grandfather said ________________.

F ▶ **6.8** Find and correct the four mistakes in this paragraph. Listen and check your answers.

At 18 years of age, Frida Kahlo was involved in an accident that changed her life forever. Her school bus hit a streetcar, and she broke her back. She had to spend many months in bed. During this time, she discovered her love of painting. Kahlo painted many self-portraits. She once told that she painted herself because she was the subject she knew best. After her long recovery, she met painter Diego Rivera. He recognized her talent and said her to keep painting. A few years later, Rivera said that he want to marry her. She told him that she is happy to become his wife and accepted his marriage proposal. It would be the beginning of a long but difficult marriage.

Frida Kahlo

SPEAKING Getting advice

A Think of two people who gave you advice. Complete the chart with notes.

	Person	Advice
1		
2		

B Work in a group. Share your advice. Can others guess who gave you the advice (and if you took it)?

Someone told me to take up acting in high school.

Was it a teacher?

Jarrett Krosoczka offers to sign a book for a young fan.

6C Inspiring lives

PRE-READING Scanning

A Work with a partner. Look at the book cover on the right. What do you think it's about?

B Scan the text to check your idea. Do you think you'd enjoy reading the book?

6.9

1 On Jarrett Krosoczka's 14th birthday, his grandparents gave him a gift—a drawing table. During dinner that night, the fortune[1] in his fortune cookie said, "You will be successful in your work." He taped it to the table.

2 Krosoczka came from a troubled family—his parents were never around, and he had few friends. His best friends at the time were the Teenage Mutant Ninja Turtles, and other characters he read about in books. When he was in the third grade, his grandparents adopted him. "They loved me so much," he says, "and they supported my creative efforts."

3 Even as a young boy, Krosoczka loved drawing and writing stories. He was lucky in that he found **encouragement** both at home and at school. One teacher in particular stood out for him: his first-grade teacher, Mrs. Alisch. "I can just remember the love that she offered us as her students," he recalls.

4 When he was 17, he volunteered at a camp for sick children called Hole in the Wall. There he met Eric, a kid with leukemia. Eric sadly didn't live to see his sixth birthday. It was an inspirational experience that Krosoczka said changed his life—it was the pivotal[2] moment that made him want to write picture books for children.

5 After graduating from art school, Krosoczka struggled to publish his work, but he never **gave up**. He eventually published his first book, *Good Night, Monkey Boy*—a story about a young, energetic boy who never wants to go to bed. His local newspaper **celebrated** the news, and he signed copies of the book at a local bookstore. Many of the people who inspired him were present at the event, including his friends, grandparents, and even several of his teachers. Mrs. Alisch, his first-grade teacher, cut in front of the line and proudly said, "I taught him how to read." It was a very special moment for Krosoczka.

6 Krosoczka is now a successful artist. His readers clearly love his books, and he receives **fan mail** from kids all over the world. Interestingly, he still draws on that same table he got on his 14th birthday, and the fortune is still taped to it.

[1] **fortune:** *n.* a prediction about your future

[2] **pivotal:** *adj.* of vital or critical importance to something

UNDERSTANDING MAIN IDEAS

Choose the best subhead for each paragraph.

1 Paragraph 3	**a** Early love of art	**b** A make-believe world
2 Paragraph 4	**a** Celebrating success	**b** A writer is born
3 Paragraph 5	**a** Success at last	**b** Funny fan mail

UNDERSTANDING SEQUENCE

Number the events from 1 to 5 in the order they happened.

_______ Krosoczka published his first book.

_______ Krosoczka began to volunteer with sick children.

_______ Krosoczka graduated from art school.

_______ Krosoczka's first-grade teacher attended his book signing.

_______ Krosoczka got a fortune cookie that said he would be successful.

UNDERSTANDING DETAILS

Match the two parts of the sentences.

1 The Teenage Mutant Ninja Turtles ○	○ adopted him.
2 Krosoczka's grandparents ○	○ taught him to read.
3 Krosoczka's parents ○	○ sent him fan mail.
4 Eric ○	○ inspired him to write children's books.
5 Mrs. Alisch ○	○ were never around.
6 Kids around the world ○	○ were his best friends.

BUILDING VOCABULARY

A Circle the correct option to complete each sentence.

1 You give **encouragement** when you want someone to _______.

a keep trying **b** stop what they're doing

2 If you **gave up** during a competition, you _______.

a quit **b** won

3 Students are likely to **celebrate** when they _______ an exam.

a pass **b** fail

4 You might send **fan mail** to _______.

a a family member **b** a famous person you like

B **CRITICAL THINKING**

Evaluating What do you think are the best things about being a children's author? What are the challenges? Discuss with a partner.

6D How a boy became an artist

TEDTALKS

JARRETT KROSOCZKA is an author and **illustrator**. In his TED Talk he describes a **compliment** he received that made a **colossal** difference in his life. His idea worth spreading is that inspiration often comes to us in unexpected ways and that we can use our own talents to inspire others.

PREVIEWING

Read the paragraph above. Circle the correct option for each sentence below. You will hear these words in the TED Talk.

1 The **illustrator** of a book is the person who (**writes it** / **draws the pictures**).

2 If you give a **compliment,** you say something (**nice** / **bad**) about someone.

3 A **colossal** failure is a (**very big** / **really small**) failure.

VIEWING

A ▶ 6.10 Watch Part 1 of the TED Talk. Circle the correct answers.

1 Who was Jack Gantos?

a an author | **b** a teacher

2 How did Gantos inspire Krosoczka?

a He complimented Krosoczka on his drawing. | **b** He helped Krosoczka write a story.

3 What did Krosoczka start to do after school?

a write letters to famous authors | **b** write his own stories

B ▶ 6.11 Watch Part 2 of the TED Talk. Check [✓] each box to show if the statement refers to Mr. Greenwood or Mr. Lynch. Some statements refer to both.

	Mr. Greenwood	Mr. Lynch
a complimented him on his drawing	☐	☐
b said he should be the school cartoonist	☐	☐
c asked him to stop drawing in class	☐	☐
d told him to forget everything he learned	☐	☐

C ▶ 6.12 Watch Part 3 of the TED Talk. Work with a partner. Explain why each thing below is important to Krosoczka.

a an email that said, "Nice work!" | **b** the date June 12, 2001 | **c** a Monkey Boy birthday cake

D CRITICAL THINKING

Inferring Why do you think Krosoczka has a framed photo of the Monkey Boy cake on his desk?

VOCABULARY IN CONTEXT

▶ 6.13 Watch the excerpts from the TED Talk. Choose the correct meaning of the words.

PRESENTATION SKILLS Using your voice effectively

> You can make your presentation clearer and more memorable by using your voice effectively. You can raise or lower your voice, stress words, vary your speed, pause, or even change your voice to indicate you're quoting another person.

A ▶ 6.14 Watch part of Jarrett Krosoczka's TED Talk. Notice how he speaks very softly when he's telling the story of the visiting author. Why do you think he does this?

B ▶ 6.15 Now watch two other TED speakers. What does each person do with his voice? Choose the correct answers.

1 **A. J. Jacobs**

a He speeds up and stresses key words. **b** He slows down and speaks very softly.

2 **Roman Mars**

a He makes his voice much higher. **b** He slows down and pauses between words.

C Work with a partner. Read the text below in different ways. How does the meaning change?

emphasizing key words **pausing at key moments** **using your grandmother's voice**

My grandmother was an inspiration to me. One day I was upset with a grade I got at school, and she said, "Just do your best. No one should expect more than that." I looked at her for a moment but didn't say a word. And deep in my heart, I knew she was right.

6E A world of inspiration

COMMUNICATE A lively dinner party

A Work alone. Write a list of people that you find inspirational. Think about people from the following categories.

political figures	athletes	musicians	entertainers
writers	artists	adventurers	scientists

B Work with a partner. Imagine you are having a small dinner party for eight people (including you and your partner). You can invite anybody you like from your lists of inspirational people. Decide on six people to invite. Give reasons for your answers.

Asking about what someone knows
Do you know ...? Have you heard of ...? Are you familiar with ...?

C Now decide on the seating plan. You want an interesting party with a lively discussion of ideas. Decide who should and shouldn't sit where.

D Work with another pair. Describe your dinner party and give reasons for your seating plan.

WRITING An inspiring person

Who do you think is inspirational? Write about them. It could be a famous person or someone you know personally. What makes the person so inspirational to you?

> My older sister Rebecca has always been a great role-model for me. She's always been very ambitious and has worked so hard to get where she is today. She's shown me that anything is possible as long as you try your best.

Presentation 2

MODEL PRESENTATION

A Complete the transcript of the presentation using the words in the box.

around	bright	gave	little	much
on	relaxed	said	showed	told

Today, I want to tell you about a person who made a huge difference in my life—my first teacher, Mrs. Daniels. When I was young, I was extremely shy and had very [1]__________________ self-confidence. I remember being so nervous on my first day at school. But Mrs. Daniels was so kind and friendly that I soon forgot about that. In that first class, Mrs. Daniels asked us all to draw a picture of ourselves to put [2]__________________ the classroom wall. She walked [3]__________________ the classroom patiently helping everyone. When she got to my desk, she looked at my picture and [4]__________________, "Wow! Look at those [5]__________________ colors! That's great!" I immediately felt [6]__________________. But that wasn't all. Mrs. Daniels was my teacher for one year, and she helped me become a lot more confident. She always praised us and encouraged us to express ourselves. She [7]__________________ us not to worry about giving wrong answers in class and [8]__________________ us how to learn from our mistakes. Even today, I still remember all the advice that Mrs. Daniels [9]__________________ me. I think without her, I would be a different person. I owe her so [10]__________________.

Thank you for listening.

B ▶ **P.2** Watch the presentation and check your answers.

C ▶ **P.2** Review the list of presentation skills from Units 1–6 below. Which does the speaker use? Check [✓] each skill used as you watch again.

The speaker …

- ☐ uses questions to signpost
- ☐ personalizes the presentation
- ☐ closes the presentation effectively
- ☐ provides background information
- ☐ numbers key points
- ☐ uses their voice effectively

YOUR TURN

A You are going to plan and give a short presentation to a partner about a great teacher you once had. Use some or all of the questions below to make some notes.

What was the teacher's name?

What did they teach?

Why were they a great teacher?

What advice did the teacher give you?

How did the teacher affect your life?

B Look at the useful phrases in the box below. Think about which ones you will need in your presentation.

Useful phrases

Giving background information:	*When I was ... / As a child ... / Before I ...*
Describing inspiration:	*changed my life / encouraged me / gave me advice / showed me / supported me / was a role-model*
Reporting what someone said:	*said that / told me that / advised me to*
Describing effects:	*I'll always remember ... / Since then, I ... I'll never forget ...*

C Work with a partner. Take turns giving your presentation using your notes. Use some of the presentation skills from Units 1–6. As you listen, check [✓] each skill your partner uses.

The speaker …

- ☐ uses questions to signpost
- ☐ personalizes the presentation
- ☐ closes the presentation effectively
- ☐ provides background information
- ☐ numbers key points
- ☐ uses their voice effectively

D Give your partner some feedback on their talk. Include two things you liked, and one thing he or she can improve.

> That was great. You used your voice really well and provided lots of background information. Next time, try to smile a bit more.

Communication Activities

1B SPEAKING

STUDENT A

A Look at this information about the Bengal tiger. Ask Student B questions to complete the chart.

Bengal tiger

Where do Bengal tigers live?

They live in …

Who are local police arresting?

They are arresting …

- **Population** 2,800
- **Where they live** ______
- **Conservation status** ______
- **Reason** ______

How people are helping

- Local police are arresting ______.
- Tour companies are offering ______.
- Park rangers are receiving additional training.

B Answer Student B's questions about the kiwi.

Kiwi

- **Population** 50,000–60,000
- **Where they live** New Zealand
- **Conservation status** threatened
- **Reason** habitat loss and predators such as cats and rats

How people are helping

- Scientists are increasing bird numbers through breeding programs.
- People are building fences to keep predators away.
- Volunteers are removing eggs from the wild and then returning the birds to the wild.

1E COMMUNICATE

STUDENT A

Indian python

Status
near threatened

Why are numbers declining?
hunting, human conflict

Why do they need saving?
- They help control pests such as rats and rabbits.
- They help keep diseases from rats spreading.

Something to consider
It is extremely rare for an Indian python to attack a human.

2E COMMUNICATE

STUDENT A

Alice is Steve's wife.
Pam is Steve's daughter.
Rex is Cindy's husband.
Susan is Cindy's daughter.
Max is Maggie's husband.
Cindy is Maggie's mother-in-law.
Cindy is John's daughter.
Max is John's grandson.

1B SPEAKING

STUDENT B

A Answer Student A's questions about the Bengal tiger.

Bengal tiger

- **Population** 2,800
- **Where they live** India, Nepal, Bangladesh
- **Conservation status** endangered
- **Reason** poaching and habitat loss

How people are helping

- Local police are arresting more poachers.
- Tour companies are offering trips to see them in the wild.
- Park rangers are receiving additional training.

B Look at this information about the kiwi. Ask Student A questions to complete the chart.

Where do kiwis live?

They live in …

How are scientists increasing bird numbers?

They're increasing bird numbers through …

Kiwi

- **Population** 50,000–60,000
- **Where they live** ____________________
- **Conservation status** ____________________
- **Reason** ____________________

How people are helping

- Scientists are increasing bird numbers through ____________________.
- People are building ____________ to keep predators away.
- Volunteers are removing eggs from the wild and then returning the birds to the wild.

1E COMMUNICATE

STUDENT B

Frégate Island beetle

Status

critically endangered

Why are numbers declining?

natural disasters, habitat loss

Why do they need saving?

- They are unique because they only live on one two-square-kilometer island.
- They are critically endangered and could become extinct very soon without help.

Something to consider

Humans have only recently started living on their island in the Indian Ocean.

2E COMMUNICATE

STUDENT B

Rex is Alice's son.
Susan is Alice's granddaughter.
Cindy is Mike's sister.
Rex is Mike's brother-in-law.
Jessica is Steve's sister.
Alice is Jessica's sister-in-law.
John is Becky's husband.
Susan is Becky's granddaughter.

1E COMMUNICATE

STUDENT C

Bluefin tuna

Status

endangered

Why are numbers declining?

popularity as food, overfishing

Why do they need saving?

- Bluefin tuna are predators. They keep smaller fish numbers in check.
- Sharks feed on bluefin tuna. Fewer tuna would mean fewer sharks.

Something to consider

It's illegal to hunt bluefin tuna in many places, but many people still do.

2E COMMUNICATE

STUDENT C

Rex is Pam's brother.
Cindy is Pam's sister-in-law.
Max is Susan's brother.
Pam is Susan's aunt.
Steve is Tom's son.
Rex is Tom's grandson.
Becky is Ed's daughter.
Susan is Ed's great-granddaughter.

1E COMMUNICATE

STUDENT D

Marine iguana

Status

vulnerable

Why are numbers declining?

introduced predators, loss of nesting areas

Why do they need saving?

- They are the only iguanas that swim, so scientists have a lot to learn about them.
- Humans introduced their predators, so we have a responsibility to protect them.

Something to consider

Many tourists go to the Galapagos Islands to see them and other unique species.

2E COMMUNICATE

STUDENT D

Cindy is Rex's wife.
Max is Rex's son.
Mike is Max's uncle.
Susan is Max's sister.
Tom is Lucy's husband.
Alice is Lucy's daughter-in-law.
Ed is Carol's husband.
Cindy is Carol's granddaughter.

5A SPEAKING

A piece of furniture at the Milan International Furniture Fair

A couch on display at the Museum of Decorative Arts, Paris

2E COMMUNICATE

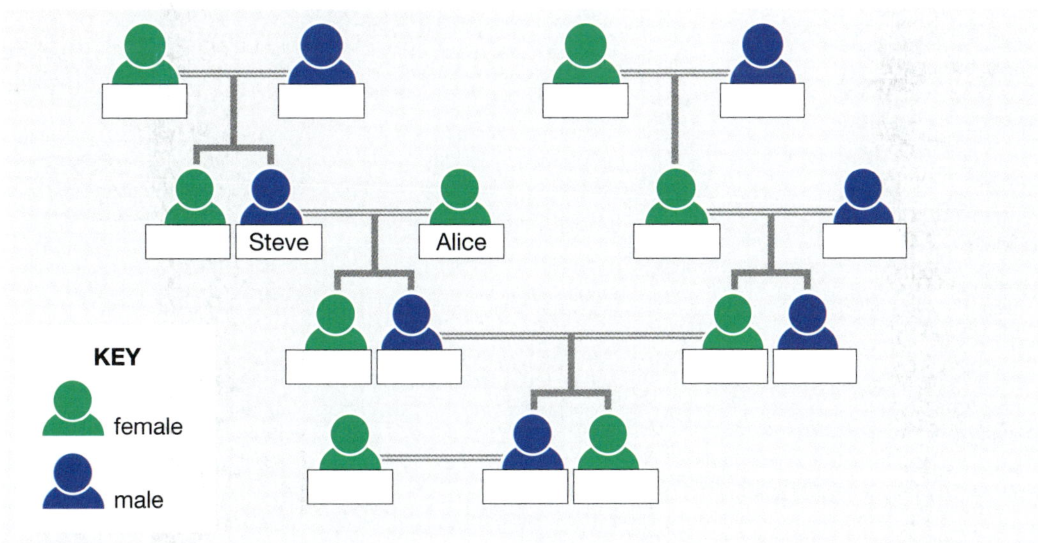

TED Talk Transcripts

Unit 1 Munir Virani: Why I love vultures

Part 1

I would like to talk to you about a very special group of animals. There are 10,000 species of birds in the world. Vultures are amongst the most threatened group of birds. When you see a vulture like this, the first thing that comes to your mind is, these are disgusting, ugly, greedy creatures that are just after your flesh, associated with politicians. I want to change that perception. I want to change those feelings you have for these birds, because they need our sympathy. They really do. And I'll tell you why.

First of all, why do they have such a bad press? When Charles Darwin went across the Atlantic in 1832 on the Beagle, he saw the turkey vulture, and he said, "These are disgusting birds with bald scarlet heads that are formed to revel in putridity." You could not get a worse insult, and that from Charles Darwin. You know, he changed his mind when he came back, and I'll tell you why. They've also be associated with Disney—personified as goofy, dumb, stupid characters.

[...] So there's two types of vultures in this planet. There are the New World vultures that are mainly found in the Americas, like the condors and the caracaras, and then the Old World vultures, where we have 16 species. From these 16, 11 of them are facing a high risk of extinction.

So why are vultures important? First of all, they provide vital ecological services. They clean up. They're our natural garbage collectors. They clean up carcasses right to the bone. They help to kill all the bacteria. They help absorb anthrax that would otherwise spread and cause huge livestock losses and diseases in other animals. Recent studies have shown that in areas where there are no vultures, carcasses take up to three to four times to decompose, and this has huge ramifications for the spread of diseases.

Part 2

So what is the problem with vultures? We have eight species of vultures that occur in Kenya, of which six are highly threatened with extinction. [...] In South Asia, in countries like India and Pakistan, four species of vultures are listed as critically endangered, which means they have less than 10 or 15 years to go extinct,

[...] So what's being done? Well, we're conducting research on these birds. We're putting transmitters on them. We're trying to determine their basic ecology, and see where they go. We can see that they travel different countries, so if you focus on a problem locally, it's not going to help you. We need to work with governments in regional levels. We're working with local communities. We're talking to them about appreciating vultures, about the need from within to appreciate these wonderful creatures and the services that they provide.

How can you help? You can become active, make noise. You can write a letter to your government and tell them that we need to focus on these very misunderstood creatures. Volunteer your time to spread the word. Spread the word. When you walk out of this room, you will be informed about vultures, but speak to your families, to your children, to your neighbors about vultures.

They are very graceful. Charles Darwin said he changed his mind because he watched them fly effortlessly without energy in the skies. Kenya, this world, will be much poorer without these wonderful species. Thank you very much.

Unit 2 A. J. Jacobs: The world's largest family reunion

Part 1

Six months ago, I got an email from a man in Israel who had read one of my books, and the email said, "You don't know me, but I'm your 12th cousin." And it said, "I have a family tree with 80,000 people on it, including you, Karl Marx, and several European aristocrats."

[...] So this email inspired me to dive into genealogy, which I always thought was a very staid and proper field, but it turns out it's going through a fascinating revolution, and a controversial one. Partly, this is because of DNA and genetic testing, but partly, it's because of the Internet. There are sites that now take the Wikipedia approach to family trees, collaboration and crowdsourcing, and what you do is, you load your family tree on, and then these sites search to see if the A. J. Jacobs in your tree is the same as the A. J. Jacobs in another tree, and if it is, then you can combine, and then you combine and combine and combine until you get these massive, mega-family trees with thousands of people on them, or even millions. I'm on something on Geni called the world family tree, which has no less than a jaw-dropping 75 million people. So that's 75 million people connected by blood or marriage, sometimes both. It's in all seven continents, including Antarctica. I'm on it. Many of you are on it, whether you know it or not, and you can see the links. Here's my cousin Gwyneth Paltrow. She has no idea I exist, but we are officially cousins. We have just 17 links between us. And there's my cousin Barack Obama. And he is my aunt's fifth great-aunt's husband's father's wife's seventh great-nephew, so practically my older brother.

[...] Now, I'm not boasting, because all of you have famous people and historical figures in your tree, because we are all connected, and 75 million may seem like a lot, but in a few years, it's quite likely we will have a family tree with all, almost all, seven billion people on Earth. But does it really matter? What's the importance?

Part 2

First, it's got scientific value. This is an unprecedented history of the human race, and it's giving us valuable data about how diseases are inherited, how people migrate, and there's a team of scientists at MIT right now studying the world family tree.

Number two, it brings history alive. I found out I'm connected to Albert Einstein, so I told my seven-year-old son that, and he was totally engaged. Now Albert Einstein is not some dead white guy with weird hair. He's Uncle Albert.

[...] Number three, interconnectedness. We all come from the same ancestor, [...] so that means we literally all are biological cousins as well, and estimates vary, but probably the farthest cousin you have on Earth is about a 50th cousin. Now, it's not just ancestors we share, descendants. If you have kids, and they have kids, look how quickly the descendants accumulate. So in 10, 12 generations, you're going to have thousands of offspring, and millions of offspring.

Number four, a kinder world. Now, I know that there are family feuds. I have three sons, so I see how they fight. But I think that there's also a human bias to treat your family a little better than strangers. I think this tree is going to be bad news for bigots, because they're going to have to realize that they are cousins with thousands of people in whatever ethnic group they happen to have issues with, and I think you look back at history, and a lot of the terrible things we've done to each other is because one group thinks another group is sub-human, and you can't do that anymore. We're not just part of the same species. We're part of the same family. We share 99.9 percent of our DNA.

Part 3

So I have all these hundreds and thousands, millions of new cousins. I thought, what can I do with this information? And that's when I decided, why not throw a party? So that's what I'm doing. And you're all invited. Next year, next summer, I will be hosting what I hope is the biggest and best family reunion in history. Thank you. I want you there. I want you there. It's going to be at the New York Hall of Science, which is a great venue,

[...] There's going to be exhibits and food, music. Paul McCartney is 11 steps away, so I'm hoping he brings his guitar. He hasn't RSVP'd yet, but fingers crossed. And there is going to be a day of speakers, of fascinating cousins.

[...] And, of course, the most important is that you, I want you guys there, and I invite you to go to GlobalFamilyReunion.org and figure out how you're on the family tree, because these are big issues, family and tribe, and I don't know all the answers, but I have a lot of smart relatives, including you guys, so together, I think we can figure it out. Only together can we solve these big problems. So from cousin to cousin, I thank you. I can't wait to see you. Goodbye.

Unit 3 Ann Morgan: My year reading a book from every country

Part 1

It's often said that you can tell a lot about a person by looking at what's on their bookshelves. What do my bookshelves say about me? Well, when I asked myself this question a few years ago, I made an alarming discovery. I'd always thought of myself as a fairly cultured, cosmopolitan sort of person. But my bookshelves told a rather different story. Pretty much all the titles on them were by British or North American authors, and there was almost nothing in translation. Discovering this massive, cultural blind spot in my reading came as quite a shock.

And when I thought about it, it seemed like a real shame. I knew there had to be lots of amazing stories out there by writers working in languages other than English. And it seemed really sad to think that my reading habits meant I would probably never encounter them. So, I decided to prescribe myself an intensive course of global reading. 2012 was set to be a very international year for the UK; it was the year of the London Olympics. And so I decided to use it as my time frame to try to read a novel, short story collection or memoir from every country in the world. And so I did. And it was very exciting and I learned some remarkable things and made some wonderful connections that I want to share with you today.

Part 2

So how on earth was I going to read the world? I was going to have to ask for help. So in October 2011, I registered my blog, ayearofreadingtheworld.com, and I posted a short appeal online. I explained who I was, how narrow my reading had been, and I asked anyone who cared to to leave a message suggesting what I might read from other parts of the planet. Now, I had no idea whether anyone would be interested, but within a few hours of me posting that appeal online, people started to get in touch. At first, it was friends and colleagues. Then it was friends of friends. And pretty soon, it was strangers.

Four days after I put that appeal online, I got a message from a woman called Rafidah in Kuala Lumpur. She said she loved the sound of my project, could she go to her local English-language bookshop and choose my Malaysian book and post it to me? I accepted enthusiastically, and a few weeks later, a package arrived containing not one, but two books—Rafidah's choice from Malaysia, and a book from Singapore that she had also picked out for me. Now, at the time, I was amazed that a stranger more than 6,000 miles away would go to such lengths to help someone she would probably never meet.

But Rafidah's kindness proved to be the pattern for that year. Time and again, people went out of their way to help me. Some took on research on my behalf, and others made detours on holidays and business trips to go to bookshops for me. It turns out, if you want to read the world, if you want to encounter it with an open mind, the world will help you.

Part 3

The books I read that year opened my eyes to many things. As those who enjoy reading will know, books have an extraordinary power to take you out of yourself and into someone else's mindset, so that, for a while at least, you look at the world through different eyes. That can be an uncomfortable experience, particularly if you're reading a book from a culture that may have quite different values to your own. But it can also be really enlightening. Wrestling with unfamiliar ideas can help clarify your own thinking. And it can also show up blind spots in the way you might have been looking at the world.

When I looked back at much of the English-language literature I'd grown up with, for example, I began to see quite how narrow a lot of it was, compared to the richness that the world has to offer. And as the pages turned, something else started to happen, too. Little by little, that long list of countries that I'd started the year with, changed from a rather dry, academic register of place names into living, breathing entities.

Now, I don't want to suggest that it's at all possible to get a rounded picture of a country simply by reading one book. But cumulatively, the stories I read that year made me more alive than ever before to the richness, diversity and complexity of our remarkable planet. It was as though the world's stories and the people who'd gone to such lengths to help me read them had made it real to me. These days, when I look at my bookshelves or consider the works on my e-reader, they tell a rather different story. It's the story of the power books have to connect us across political, geographical, cultural, social, religious divides. It's the tale of the potential human beings have to work together.

[...] And I hope many more people will join me. If we all read more widely, there'd be more incentive for publishers to translate more books, and we would all be richer for that.

Thank you.

Unit 4 Daria van den Bercken: Why I take the piano on the road ... and in the air

Part 1

Recently, I flew over a crowd of thousands of people in Brazil playing music by George Frideric Handel. I also drove along the streets of Amsterdam, again playing music by this same composer. Let's take a look.

[Music: George Frideric Handel, "Allegro." Performed by Daria van den Bercken.]

[Video] Daria van den Bercken: I live there on the third floor. [In Dutch] I live there on the corner. I actually live there, around the corner ... and you'd be really welcome.

Man: [In Dutch] Does that sound like fun?

Child: [In Dutch] Yes!

Daria van den Bercken: All this was a real magical experience for hundreds of reasons. Now you may ask, why have I done these things? They're not really typical for a musician's day-to-day life. Well, I did it because I fell in love with the music and I wanted to share it with as many people as possible.

It started a couple of years ago. I was sitting at home on the couch with the flu and browsing the Internet a little, when I found out that Handel had written works for the keyboard. Well, I was surprised. I did not know this. So I downloaded the sheet music and started playing. And what happened next was that I entered this state of pure, unprejudiced amazement. It was an experience of being totally in awe of the music, and I had not felt that in a long time. It might be easier to relate to this when you hear it. The first piece that I played through started like this. [Music] Well this sounds very melancholic, doesn't it? And I turned the page and what came next was this. [Music] Well, this sounds very energetic, doesn't it? So within a couple of minutes, and the piece isn't even finished yet, I experienced two very contrasting characters: beautiful melancholy and sheer energy. And I consider these two elements to be vital human expressions. And the purity of the music makes you hear it very effectively.

Part 2

I've given a lot of children's concerts for children of seven and eight years old, and whatever I play, whether it's Bach, Beethoven, even Stockhausen, or some jazzy music, they are open to hear it, really willing to listen, and they are comfortable doing so. And when classes come in with children who are just a few years older, 11, 12, I felt that I sometimes already had trouble in reaching them like that. The complexity of the music does become an issue, and actually the opinions of others—parents, friends, media—they start to count. But the young ones, they don't question their own opinion. They are in this constant state of wonder, and I do firmly believe that we can keep listening like these seven-year-old children, even when growing up. And that is why I have played not only in the concert hall but also on the street, online, in the air: to feel that state of wonder, to truly listen, and to listen without prejudice. And I would like to invite you to do so now. [music]

Thank you.

Unit 5 Roman Mars: The worst-designed thing you've never noticed

Part 1

I know what you're thinking: "Why does that guy get to sit down?" That's because this is radio.

I tell radio stories about design, and I report on all kinds of stories: buildings and toothbrushes and mascots and wayfinding and fonts. My mission is to get people to engage with the design that they care about so they begin to pay attention to all forms of design.

[...] And few things give me greater joy than a well-designed flag. Yeah! Happy 50th anniversary on your flag, Canada. It is beautiful, gold standard. Love it. I'm kind of obsessed with flags. Sometimes I bring up the topic of flags, and people are like, "I don't care about flags," and then we start talking about flags, and trust me, 100 percent of people care about flags. There's just something about them that works on our emotions.

[...] Okay. So when I moved back to San Francisco in 2008, I researched its flag, because I had never seen it in the previous eight years I lived there. And I found it, I am sorry to say, sadly lacking. I know. It hurts me, too.

Part 2

Narrator: The five basic principles of flag design. Number one.

Flag expert, Ted Kaye: Keep it simple. Narrator: Number two. TK: Use meaningful symbolism.

Narrator: Number three. TK: Use two to three basic colors.

Narrator: Number four. TK: No lettering or seals.

Narrator: Never use writing of any kind. TK: Because you can't read that at a distance.

Narrator: Number five. TK: And be distinctive.

Roman Mars: All the best flags tend to stick to these principles. And like I said before, most country flags are okay. But here's the thing: if you showed this list of principles to any designer of almost anything, they would say these principles—simplicity, deep meaning, having few colors or being thoughtful about colors, uniqueness, don't have writing you can't read—all those principles apply to them, too.

[...] But here's the trick: If you want to design a great flag, a kickass flag like Chicago's or D.C.'s, which also has a great flag, start by drawing a one-by-one-and-a-half-inch rectangle on a piece of paper. Your design has to fit within that tiny rectangle. Here's why.

TK: A three-by-five-foot flag on a pole 100 feet away looks about the same size as a one-by-one-and-a-half-inch rectangle seen about 15 inches from your eye. You'd be surprised at how compelling and simple the design can be when you hold yourself to that limitation.

RM: Meanwhile, back in San Francisco. Is there anything we can do?

TK: I like to say that in every bad flag there's a good flag trying to get out. The way to make San Francisco's flag a good flag is to take the motto off because you can't read that at a distance. Take the name off, and the border might even be made thicker, so it's more a part of the flag. And I would simply take the phoenix and make it a great big element in the middle of the flag.

RM: But the current phoenix, that's got to go.

TK: I would simplify or stylize the phoenix. Depict a big, wide-winged bird coming out of flames. Emphasize those flames.

RM: So this San Francisco flag was designed by Frank Chimero based on Ted Kaye's suggestions. I don't know what he would do if we was completely unfettered and didn't follow those guidelines. Fans of my radio show and podcast, they've heard me complain about bad flags. They've sent me other suggested designs. This one's by Neil Mussett. Both are so much better. And I think if they were adopted, I would see them around the city.

Part 3

TK: Often when city leaders say, "We have more important things to do than worry about a city flag," my response is, "If you had a great city flag, you would have a banner for people to rally under to face those more important things."

[...] So maybe all the city flags can be as inspiring as Hong Kong or Portland or Trondheim, and we can do away with all the bad flags like San Francisco, Milwaukee, Cedar Rapids, and finally, when we're all done, we can do something about Pocatello, Idaho, considered by the North American Vexillological Association as the worst city flag in North America. Yeah. That thing has a trademark symbol on it, people. That hurts me just to look at. Thank you so much for listening.

Unit 6 Jarrett J. Krosoczka: How a boy became an artist

Part 1

When I was in the third grade, a monumental event happened. An author visited our school, Jack Gantos. A published author of books came to talk to us about what he did for a living. And afterwards, we all went back to our classrooms and we drew our own renditions of his main character, Rotten Ralph. And suddenly the author appeared in our doorway, and I remember him sort of sauntering down the aisles, going from kid to kid looking at the desks, not saying a word. But he stopped next to my desk, and he tapped on my desk, and he said, "Nice cat." And he wandered away. Two words that made a colossal difference in my life. When I was in the third grade, I wrote a book for the first time, "The Owl Who Thought He Was The Best Flyer."

[...] So I loved writing so much that I'd come home from school, and I would take out pieces of paper, and I would staple them together, and I would fill those blank pages with words and pictures just because I loved using my imagination. And so these characters would become my friends. There was an egg, a tomato, a head of lettuce and a pumpkin, and they all lived in this refrigerator city, and in one of their adventures they went to a haunted house that was filled with so many dangers like an evil blender who tried to chop them up, an evil toaster who tried to kidnap the bread couple, and an evil microwave who tried to melt their friend who was a stick of butter.

Part 2

So how did I make friends? I drew funny pictures of my teachers—and I passed them around. Well, in English class, in ninth grade, my friend John, who was sitting next to me, laughed a little bit too hard. Mr. Greenwood was not pleased. He instantly saw that I was the cause of the commotion, and for the first time in my life, I was sent to the hall, and I thought, "Oh no, I'm doomed. My grandfather's just going to kill me." And he came out to the hallway and he said, "Let me see the paper." And I thought, "Oh no. He thinks it's a note." And so I took this picture, and I handed it to him. And we sat in silence for that brief moment, and he said to me, "You're really talented." "You're really good. You know, the school newspaper needs a new cartoonist, and you should be the cartoonist. Just stop drawing in my class." So my parents never found out about it. I didn't get in trouble.

[...] I kept making comics, and at the Worcester Art Museum, I was given the greatest piece of advice by any educator I was ever given. Mark Lynch, he's an amazing teacher and he's still a dear friend of mine, and I was 14 or 15, and I walked into his comic book class halfway through the course, and I was so excited, I was beaming. I had this book that was how to draw comics in the Marvel way, and it taught me how to draw superheroes, how to draw a woman, how to draw muscles just the way they were supposed to be if I were to ever draw for X-Men or Spiderman. And all the color just drained from his face, and he looked at me, and he said, "Forget everything you learned." And I didn't understand. He said, "You have a great style. Celebrate your own style. Don't draw the way you're being told to draw. Draw the way you're drawing and keep at it, because you're really good."

Part 3

I graduated from RISD. My grandparents were very proud, and I moved to Boston, and I set up shop. I set up a studio and I tried to get published. I would send out my books. I would send out hundreds of postcards to editors and art directors, but they would go unanswered.

[...] Now, I used to work the weekends at the Hole in the Wall off-season programming to make some extra money as I was trying to get my feet off the ground, and this kid who was just this really hyper kid, I started calling him "Monkey Boy," and I went home and wrote a book called "Good Night, Monkey Boy." And I sent out one last batch of postcards. And I received an email from an editor at Random House with a subject line, "Nice work!" Exclamation point. "Dear Jarrett, I received your postcard. I liked your art, so I went to your website and I'm wondering if you ever tried writing any of your own stories, because I really like your art and it looks like there are some stories that go with them. Please let me know if you're ever in New York City." And this was from an editor at Random House Children's Books. So the next week I "happened" to be in New York. And I met with this editor, and I left New York for a contract for my first book, "Good Night, Monkey Boy," which was published on June 12, 2001.

[...] And then something happened that changed my life. I got my first piece of significant fan mail, where this kid loved Monkey Boy so much that he wanted to have a Monkey Boy birthday cake. For a two-year-old, that is like a tattoo. You know? You only get one birthday per year. And for him, it's only his second. And I got this picture, and I thought, "This picture is going to live within his consciousness for his entire life. He will forever have this photo in his family photo albums." So that photo, since that moment, is framed in front of me while I've worked on all of my books.

[...] And I get the most amazing fan mail, and I get the most amazing projects, and the biggest moment for me came last Halloween. The doorbell rang and it was a trick-or-treater dressed as my character. It was so cool.

Grammar Summary

UNIT 1: Simple present and present continuous

I'm reading a book about pandas. She's volunteering at the animal shelter. They're studying global warming. I'm not working on my report right now. She isn't supporting our cause. They aren't studying owls. Is the weather changing around here? Yes, it is. / No, it isn't. Are panda numbers declining? Yes, they are. / No, they aren't.	We use the present continuous to talk about … • events in progress. *The polar bear is hunting for seals.* • changing situations. *Polar bear numbers are decreasing.* We use the simple present to talk about … • habits and routines. *Seals hunt penguins.* • things that are always true. *Polar bears have thick fur.*

UNIT 2: Future forms

I'm (not) going to be at the reunion. He's (not) going to come on Friday. They're (not) going to stay long. Who are you going to bring? What time is your sister going to come? How long are your parents going to stay?	We use both *be going to* and the present continuous to talk about future arrangements. • *I'm going to see my family this weekend.* • *I'm seeing my family this weekend.* We use *be going to* when we want to talk about intentions in the more distant future. • *I'm going to be a dentist when I'm older.*

UNIT 3: Relative clauses

It's about a young boy. He's a wizard. It's about a young boy who's a wizard. He has some friends. They help him. He has some friends who help him. I'm reading a book. It's really good. I'm reading a book that's really good. That is the place. He grew up there. That is the place where he grew up.	A relative clause can begin with a pronoun that acts as its subject. The verb agrees with the subject. • *It's about a wizard who lives at a school.* • *It's about wizards who live at a school.* We use *who* to add details to people, *that* to add details to things, and *where* to add details to places. • *Draco is the one who doesn't like Harry.* • *Hedwig is an owl that helps Harry.* • *Hogwarts is the school where he studies.*

UNIT 4: Countable and uncountable nouns

Countable nouns How many songs can you play on your guitar? I know a lot of / some / a few songs. I don't know many / any songs. There were too many people there. ***Uncountable nouns*** How much rock music do you have? I have a lot of / some / a little rock music. I don't have much / any pop music. You have too much pop music.	Countable nouns can be singular or plural. Uncountable nouns are always singular. • *Did you buy one ticket or two tickets?* • *All their music is very unusual.* We can use *many* and *a few* before countable nouns and *much* and *a little* before uncountable nouns. We can use *a lot of, some, (not) any*, before either. • *He doesn't have many / a lot of friends.* • *He doesn't have much / a lot of money.*

UNIT 5: Prepositions of place

I live in a small house. The living room is at the top of the stairs. The door is at the bottom of the stairs. There is a large blue rug on the floor. It has a red border around it. There is a bookshelf on the left / on the right. A table is to the left of / to the right of the sofa. There is a TV in front of the sofa. There is a window behind the sofa. There is a garage next to my house. I park my car inside the garage. There are some trees between my house and my neighbor's house.	We can use prepositions to describe the location of things. • *There is a picture on the wall.* • *Your coat is in the closet.* • *There is a lamp next to the sofa.* Some prepositions have opposites. • *The plant is to the left of the table.* • *The table is to the right of the plant.* • *The table is in front of the sofa.* • *The sofa is behind the table.*

UNIT 6: Reported speech

"I need help." I said (that) I needed help. I told him (that) I needed help. "Stop." I told him to stop. "Don't continue." I told him not to continue. "I want an ice cream." She said (that) she wanted an ice cream. "I don't understand." He said (that) he didn't understand.	When we use *tell*, we name the person that is spoken to. With *say*, we do not. • *He told me (that) he was sorry.* • *He said (that) he was sorry.* We use *tell someone to* when we want to report orders or advice. • *She told me to be quiet.* *He told her not to worry.* Present tense verbs often change to a past tense form in reported speech. • *"I believe in you."* *He said that he believed in me.*

Acknowledgements

The Author and Publisher would like to thank the following teaching professionals for their valuable input during the development of this series:

Coleeta Paradise Abdullah, Certified Training Center; **Tara Amelia Arntsen**, Northern State University; **Estela Campos**; **Federica Castro**, Pontificia Universidad Católica Madre y Maestra; **Amy Cook**, Bowling Green State University; **Carrie Cheng**, School of Continuing and Professional Studies, the University of Hong Kong; **Mei-ho Chiu**, Soochow University; **Anthony Sean D'Amico**, SDH Institute; **Wilder Yesid Escobar Almeciga**, Universidad El Bosque; **Rosa E. Vasquez Fernandez**, English for International Communication; **Touria Ghaffari**, The Beekman School; **Rosario Giraldez**, Alianza Cultural Uruguay Estados Unidos; **William Haselton**, NC State University; **Yu Huichun**, Macau University of Science and Technology; **Michelle Kim**, TOPIA Education; **Jay Klaphake**, Kyoto University of Foreign Studies; **Kazuteru Kuramoto**, Keio Senior High School; **Michael McCollister**, Feng Chia University; **Jennifer Meldrum**, EC English Language Centers; **Holly Milkowart**, Johnson County Community College; **Nicholas Millward**, Australian Centre for Education; **Stella Maris Palavecino**, Buenos Aires English House; **Youngsun Park**, YBM; **Adam Parmentier**, Mingdao High School; **Jennie Popp**, Universidad Andrés Bello; **Terri Rapoport**, ELS Educational Services; **Erich Rose**, Auburn University; **Yoko Sakurai**, Aichi University; **Mark D. Sheehan**, Hannan University; **DongJin Shin**, Hankuk University of Foreign Studies; **Shizuka Tabara**, Kobe University; **Jeffrey Taschner**, AUA Language Center; **Hadrien Tournier**, Berlitz Corporation; **Rosa Vasquez**, JFK Institute; **Jindarat De Vleeschauwer**, Chiang Mai University; **Tamami Wada**, Chubu University; **Colin Walker**, Myongii University; **Elizabeth Yoon**, Hanyang University; **Keiko Yoshida**, Konan University

And special thanks to: **Tony Gainsford, Neil Glover, Fredrik Hiebert, Mary Kadera, Sarah Lafferty, Ken Lejtenyi, Joel Sartore, Barton Seaver, Claire Street, Madeleine Thien**

Credits

Photo Credits

Cover © Patrick Bingham Hall, **3** Thomas J. Abercrombie/National Geographic Creative, **4** (tl) © Munir Virani, (tr) © Marla Aufmuth/TED, (cl) © James Duncan Davidson/TED, (cr) © Handel At The Piano, (bl) © Bret Hartman/TED, (br) Boston Globe/Getty Images, **6** (tl1) Joel Sartore, National Geographic Photo ARK/National Geographic Creative, (tl2) Joel Sartore/ National Geographic Creative, (cl1) Thomas J. Abercrombie /National Geographic Creative, (cl2) PeopleImages.com/DigitalVision/Getty Images, (bl1) The Washington Post/Getty Images, (bl2) Greg Dale/National Geographic Creative, **10–11** © James Duncan Davidson/ TED, **12** © Michael Brands/TED, **13** © Munir Virani, **14** Joel Sartore, National Geographic Photo ARK/National Geographic Creative, **15** Joel Sartore/National Geographic Creative, **17** Gallo Images/Getty Images, **18** Joel Sartore/National Geographic Creative, **20** © TED, **21** Joel Sartore/National Geographic Creative, **22** (tl) Joel Sartore, National Geographic Photo ARK/National Geographic Creative, (tr) Danita Delimont Creative/Alamy Stock Photo, (cl) Brian J. Skerry/National Geographic Creative, (cr) Joel Sartore/National Geographic Creative, **23** © Marla Aufmuth/TED, **24** Blend Images/Alamy Stock Photo, **25** © Ken Lejtenyi, **27** Stacy Gold/National Geographic Creative, **28** Diana Haronis dianasphotoart.com/Moment Select/Getty Images, **30** © Marla Aufmuth/TED, **31** © Elana Goodridge, **32** Blend Images/Alamy Stock Photo, **33** © James Duncan Davidson/TED, **34** Thomas J. Abercrombie/National Geographic Creative, **35** Ullstein Bild/Getty Images, **37** © Harper Collins Publishers. All rights reserved, **38** (tr) © Geopoetika, (cl) © Penguin Books India, (br) © Milkweed Editions, a nonprofit, literary publisher. All rights reserved, **40–41** © James Duncan Davidson/TED, **42** © Hogarth, an imprint of the Crown Publishing Group, a division of Penguin Random House LLC, New York. All rights reserved, **43** © Cengage Learning, **45** © Handel at The Piano, **46** PeopleImages.com/DigitalVision/Getty Images, **47** Hiroyuki Ito/Hulton Archive/Getty Images, **49** Lucy Nicholson/Reuters, **50** Hill Street Studios/Blend Images/Getty Images, **52–53** © James Duncan Davidson/TED, **54** Caroline von Tuempling/ The Image Bank/Getty Images, **55** © Bret Hartman/TED, **56** Nikki Kahn/The Washington Post/Getty Images, **57** © Sarah Lafferty, **59** (tl) Squareplum/Shutterstock.com, (tc) Geff Reis/ AGE fotostock, (tr) Manon van Os/Shutterstock.com, (cr) ollo/E+/Getty Images, **60** Daniel Stein/iStock/Getty Images Plus/Getty Images, **62** (tr) © Bret Hartman/TED, (cl) Sagid/Shutterstock.com, (cr) Wasan Ritthawon/Shutterstock.com, **64** (tl) Wasan Ritthawon/ Shutterstock.com, (tc) Wasan Ritthawon/Shutterstock.com, (tr) Juergen Priewe/Dreamstime. com, **65** Essdras M Suarez/The Boston Globe/Getty Images, **66** Greg Dale/National Geographic Creative, **67** John B. Carnett/Bonnier Corporation/Getty Images, **69** Bettmann/ Getty Images, **70** (t) John Leyba/The Denver Post/Getty Images, (cr) © Dragonfly Books, **72–73** © TED, **75** © Cengage Learning, **141** (tl) Steve Winter/National Geographic Creative, (cl) (bc) Joel Sartore, National Geographic Photo Ark/National Geographic Creative, **142** (tl) Joel Sartore, National Geographic Photo Ark/National Geographic Creative, (cl) Steve Winter/National Geographic Creative, (bc) Danita Delimont Creative/Alamy Stock Photo, **144** Brian J. Skerry/National Geographic Creative, **146** (cl) Joel Sartore/National Geographic Creative, **147** (t) Giuseppe Cacace/AFP/Getty Images, (c) Fred Dufour/AFP/Getty Images

Illustration & Infographic Credits

16, 26, 36, 48, 58, 68 emc design

Data sources for infographics: **16** www.worldwildlife.org, **26** www.guinnessworldrecords.com, **36** www.goodreads.com, **58** www.familynamesonline.com, **68** www.raconteur.net

Text Credits

18 Source of data: "Vultures are revolting. Here's why we need to save them": ngm. nationalgeographic.com, January 2016, "Why Africa's vultures are collapsing toward extinction": news.nationalgeographic.com, July 2016, **50** Adapted from "Why does music feel so good?": phenomena.nationalgeographic.com, April 2013

Keynote 2

Workbook

David Bohlke
Eunice Yeates

NATIONAL GEOGRAPHIC LEARNING | CENGAGE Learning

Australia • Brazil • Mexico • Singapore • United Kingdom • United States

Contents

Scope and Sequence

UNIT	LESSON A	LESSON B
TITLE	VOCABULARY LISTENING	LANGUAGE FOCUS LISTENING FOCUS
1 Protectors	Types of animals Monarch butterflies	Discussing conservation status Recognizing /s/ and /z/ sounds
2 Family Connections	Extended family A member of the family	Discussing plans and arrangements Reduction of *going to* and *want to*
3 Global Stories	Genres of fiction My favorite book	Describing stories Dropped /v/ sound in *of*
4 Music	Music Music preferences	Discussing types of music Stress patterns
5 Good Design	Design elements A designer's advice	Discussing elements of design Dropped /d/ and /t/
6 Inspiration	Sources of inspiration My inspiration	Discussing inspirational people Pausing after commas

LESSON C VOCABULARY BUILDING	LESSON D TED PLAYLIST	LESSON E WRITING
Collocations with *common*	How poachers became caretakers How do you save a shark you know nothing about? The dawn of de-extinction. Are you ready?	An endangered species
Prefix *gen-*	A family tree for humanity The search for humanity's roots A dig for humanity's origins	An invitation
Suffix *-ous*	Finding the story inside the painting How books can open your mind What fear can teach us	A book recommendation
Phrasal verbs with *turn*	Home is a song I've always remembered The violin—and my dark night of the soul A-rhythm-etic. The math behind the beats	A favorite song
Suffix *-ize*	The first secret of design is ... noticing Great design is serious, not solemn Can design save newspapers?	My country's flag
Collocations with *effort*	Every kid needs a champion Kids, take charge Why lunch ladies are heroes	An inspiring person

1 Protectors

1A

VOCABULARY Types of animals

A Match each word in the box to its definition.

amphibian	bird	fish	insect	mammal	reptile

1 ____________ An animal that feeds its young with milk from the mother.
2 ____________ An animal that has feathers and can usually fly.
3 ____________ A cold-blooded animal that lays eggs on land.
4 ____________ A very small animal that has six legs.
5 ____________ An animal that first lives in water and can later breathe on land.
6 ____________ An animal that cannot survive outside water.

B Complete the sentences using the words in the box.

bee	frog	penguin	snake

1 I'm a bird, but I can't fly. I'm a great swimmer, though! I'm black and white. I'm a ____________.

2 I'm an amphibian. I have short front legs and long back legs. I usually live near water. I can hop and jump and swim. I'm a ____________.

3 I'm a reptile. I have a long body and strong muscles, but I have no arms or legs. I'm a ____________.

4 I'm an insect. I get my food from flowers, and I use it to make honey. I live in most parts of the world. I'm a ____________.

LISTENING Monarch butterflies

A ▶ 1.1 Listen. What is the talk mainly about?

- **a** why monarch butterflies travel very long distances
- **b** the life cycle of the monarch butterfly
- **c** the problems faced by monarch butterflies

B ▶ 1.1 Listen again. Circle the best answer.

1 Where do most monarch butterflies go for the winter?

a Canada **b** California **c** Mexico

2 The monarch butterfly population began to decline ______.

a in 2016 **b** over 20 years ago **c** within the last 20 years

3 Which of these is **not** a cause for the decline in the monarch butterfly population?

a climate change **b** human activities **c** an increase in predators

4 What is the monarch butterfly's conservation status now?

a near-threatened **b** threatened **c** endangered

COMMUNICATION Talking about endangered animals

A Complete the conversation. Number the sentences (**1–7**) in the correct order.

a ______ Well, I guess my first question is, are giant tortoises an endangered species?

b ______ Oh, no! That's not very many. I hope conservationists can find a way to protect them soon.

c __1__ Hey, I'm working on a paper about giant tortoises. Do you think you could help me out?

d ______ Sure, how can I help?

e ______ Well, I'm not sure of the exact number, but I think there are only about 2,000 of them left.

f ______ Hmm... No, they aren't. But they are listed as vulnerable.

g ______ Really? So how many giant tortoises still live in the wild?

B Complete the conversation using the information in the box.

> Many chimpanzees have died of disease, but the biggest threats to their survival are hunting and poaching. Their population has declined to around 170,000–300,000 in the wild.
>
> Status: ENDANGERED

A: What are you reading about?

B: I'm reading about [1] ______________. It says they're [2] ______________.

A: That's terrible! Why?

B: Well, it's mostly because of [3] ______________.

A: How many are there left in the wild?

B: Only [4] ______________.

A: They're amazing animals. I really hope we find a way to save them soon.

1B

LANGUAGE FOCUS Discussing conservation status

A Correct the mistakes in the sentences below.

1 These days, awareness of endangered species ~~improves~~. is improving
2 Still, many of the world's wildlife populations decreases.
3 There's good news and bad news: Giant panda numbers increase but polar bear numbers are decline.
4 Others are help in conservation efforts.
5 Does the conservation status of an animal making a difference to those fighting to protect it?
6 Is your government do anything to change the situation?

B ▶ 1.2 Circle the correct words to complete the interview. Then listen and check your answers.

A: What is the World Wildlife Fund?
B: The World Wildlife Fund, or WWF, is an international organization. It [1] (**is protecting** / **protects**) wildlife and the environment.
A: Is the World Wildlife Fund [2] (**works** / **working on**) projects in many countries?
B: [3] (**Yes, it is** / **No, it isn't**). There are WWF projects in more than 100 countries.
A: Does the WWF [4] (**get** / **getting**) all its money from the government?
B: No it doesn't. It [5] (**is getting** / **gets**) some funding from governments, some from corporations, and most from public donations.

LISTENING FOCUS Recognizing /s/ and /z/ sounds

A ▶ 1.3 Most plural words in English end with *s*. The letter *s* can be pronounced in different ways. Listen and repeat what you hear.

/s/ parents	sleeps	weeks	books
/z/ kids	dogs	days	needs

B ▶ 1.4 Listen. Circle each sound that you hear.

1 ants	**a** /s/	**b** /z/	**2** butterflies	**a** /s/	**b** /z/	**3** cats	**a** /s/	**b** /z/
4 bees	**a** /s/	**b** /z/	**5** pandas	**a** /s/	**b** /z/	**6** tigers	**a** /s/	**b** /z/

C ▶ 1.5 Write each word under the correct heading. Then listen and check your answers.

elephants **eyes** **frogs** **hops** **monkeys** **penguins**

/s/	/z/

1C

READING

Read the passage and answer the questions.

The pig-like snout is used to breathe when underwater and sense prey in muddy waters.

1 Turtles are among the oldest creatures in the world; the turtle family is over 200 million years old. But many turtle species are already extinct, while others are endangered, critically endangered, or vulnerable. One vulnerable species is the pig-nosed turtle.

2 Pig-nosed turtles live in rivers in northern Australia and southern Papua New Guinea. Some people say they are ugly creatures because their noses look like a pig's snout, or nose. But these strange noses are actually very useful. Their design makes it easier for the turtle to swim and to find prey. Unlike all other freshwater turtles, pig-nosed turtles have flippers instead of feet, which means they can swim like sea turtles.

3 In 2011, the pig-nosed turtle was facing extinction. Between 1981 and 2011, its population dropped by over 50 percent. Unluckily for the pig-nosed turtle, its eggs and meat were a common source of food for communities in Papua New Guinea and Indonesia. In Australia, the cause was loss of habitat due to agriculture, mining, and fishing. Another major problem was the illegal global trade of these animals as pets.

4 But there is positive news. Agricultural methods are changing in Australia. The Indonesian government and the Convention on International Trade in Endangered Species (CITES) now protect the species. In recent years, thousands of pig-nosed turtles have been rescued from poachers. They may not be beautiful, but pig-nosed turtles are important animals, and we must continue to stop their decline.

A What is the main idea of the passage?

a how pig-nosed turtles have been rescued from poachers

b why pig-nosed turtles almost became extinct

c vulnerable pig-nosed turtles are now a lot better protected

B Circle the correct words to complete the sentences.

1 The conservation status of the pig-nosed turtle is (**endangered** / **vulnerable**).

2 Pig-nosed turtles are (**similar to** / **different from**) other freshwater turtles. They have flippers instead of feet to help them swim.

3 By 2011, the number of pig-nosed turtles had declined by more than half because of (**human activities** / **natural causes**).

4 We can infer from the last paragraph that conservation efforts (**are** / **are not**) working.

LISTENING

A ▶ 1.6 Listen. What kind of recording is this?

a a news article **b** a personal opinion **c** a public lecture

B ▶ 1.6 Listen again. Check [✓] the statements the speaker would most likely agree with.

1 People are responsible for the extinction of animals. ☐

2 Pig-nosed turtles are special because there are no other turtles like them. ☐

3 These turtles deserve to be treated better than they have been treated. ☐

4 We hear about pig-nosed turtles in the news all the time. ☐

5 Pig-nosed turtles are extremely ugly. ☐

6 Animals that are cuter than pig-nosed turtles get more attention. ☐

C **CRITICAL THINKING** Circle the statement you most agree with. Give a reason for your answer.

a People would be more interested in protecting pig-nosed turtles if they were cute.

b There should be more international awareness of the pig-nosed turtle and its problems.

c Local communities should be allowed to have pig-nosed turtles as a source of food.

Reason: ____

____

VOCABULARY BUILDING

A Complete the sentences using the words in the box.

common	communities	government	treated	worried

1 It is quite ______________ to hear about the illegal smuggling of wildlife these days.

2 The ______________ needs to enforce harsher laws as a deterrent.

3 Local ______________ need to keep a watchful eye for poaching or smuggling activities.

4 Many NGOs are ______________ that the problem may be more serious than it appears to be.

5 Animals that are rescued from poachers or smugglers are often ______________ before being released back into the wild.

B Read the passage. Then match each phrase in **bold** to its definition.

Bees are essential for **the common good**. It's **common knowledge** that bees pollinate crops and wildflowers. Without bees, plants can't survive. So, it's **common sense** to change agricultural policies and protect bees.

1 the ability to think reasonably and to make good decisions: ______________

2 something that benefits everyone: ______________

3 something that is known by everyone (or by most people): ______________

1D

TED PLAYLIST

Animals gathering at a watering hole in Etosha National Park, Namibia

HOW POACHERS BECAME CARETAKERS

John Kasaona talks about several difficult issues that both humans and animals have faced in his home country of Namibia. He describes some unusual conservation projects in which local communities, and even former poachers, are successfully protecting wildlife in their area.

HOW DO YOU SAVE A SHARK YOU KNOW NOTHING ABOUT?

They're the second largest fish in the world, they're almost extinct, and we know almost nothing about them. In this talk, marine biologist Simon Berrow describes Ireland's fascinating basking shark and the exceptionally low-tech methods he uses to study them.

THE DAWN OF DE-EXTINCTION. ARE YOU READY?

Stewart Brand recognizes our duty to protect endangered animals because we are responsible for making many species disappear forever. But is it really "forever"? He proposes a radical method to change the finality of extinction.

A Circle the best title for the playlist.

a Filming Endangered Species **b** Unusual Ways of Saving Animals **c** The Dangers of Poaching

B Answer the questions.

1 Which speaker is trying to study an animal that scientists know very little about?

____

2 Who works on the conservation projects described by John Kasaona?

____

3 According to Stewart Brand, why should human beings protect endangered species?

____

C Circle the correct answers.

1 A former president is someone who ______.
   a is president now **b** was president in the past

2 Something that is exceptional is ______.
   a out of the ordinary **b** boring and dull

3 If an idea is radical, it is ______.
   a old-fashioned **b** new and very different

D Decide which talk you most want to watch. Watch it online at www.ted.com.

1E

WRITING An endangered species

A Read the sample passage about an animal that needs protection.

In the first paragraph, state the animal you think needs protection and its conservation status.

One example of an animal that needs our protection is the tiger. Tigers are an endangered species, and some species of tigers are already extinct.

Begin the second paragraph by introducing a new point (or points).

One important thing to consider is that tigers are facing extinction because of us. For example, we are forcing them to live closer to human communities. Tigers are killed when they come into contact with people. Poaching is another big problem.

Support your point(s) with reasons or examples.

Tigers are a vital part of our wildlife. We are losing too many of these wonderful creatures, and we have to save them before it's too late.

Try to use the simple present and present continuous tenses, as well as some new words from this unit.

B Think of another animal that needs protection. Answer the questions to plan your passage.

1 Which animal do you think needs protection?

2 What is the animal's conservation status?

3 What are the threats to this animal's survival?

4 What is your conclusion?

C Now write your passage. Then complete the checklist below.

- ☐ Did you use correct spelling and punctuation?
- ☐ Did you use the simple present and the present continuous tenses?
- ☐ Did you use some new words from this unit?
- ☐ Did you support your points with reasons or examples?

2 Family Connections

2A

VOCABULARY Extended family

A Write the opposite male or female form for each family member using the words in the box. Two are extra.

brother-in-law	**granddaughter**	**grandchild**	**grandfather**
mother-in-law	**nephew**	**niece**	**son-in-law**

1 daughter-in-law ____________ **4** sister-in-law ____________

2 niece ____________ **5** father-in-law ____________

3 grandmother ____________ **6** grandson ____________

B Complete the sentences using the words in **A**.

1 I'm married to Kate. Kate's mother is Ellen. Ellen is my ________________________.

2 My father is Ken. His father is Hank. Hank is my ________________________.

3 My daughter is Emiko. Her husband is Jun. Jun is my ________________________.

4 My brother has a daughter named Ashley. Ashley is my ________________________.

5 Pablo is my sister's husband. Pablo is my ________________________.

6 My sister and her husband have a son named Matt. Matt is my ________________________.

7 My son's wife is going to have a baby. The baby will be my first ________________________.

LISTENING A member of the family

A ▶ 2.1 Listen. Number the family members the speaker mentions (**1**–**4**) in the correct order.

a ______ his daughter **c** ______ his brother-in-law

b ______ his wife **d** ______ his wife's parents

B ▶ 2.1 Listen again. Complete the sentences using information from the talk.

1 The house belongs to Rebecca's ________________ and ________________.

2 Casey is the man's ________________.

3 Caitlin is Casey's ________________.

COMMUNICATION Talking about family

A Complete the conversation. Number the sentences (**1**–**6**) in the correct order.

a ______ Wow, you must miss them a lot. Are they going to stay at your place?

b ______ Let's see ... on Saturday night, I'm taking them out for dinner, then we're going to catch a movie.

c ______ So what are your plans for them?

d ______ Well, my parents are coming for a visit on Saturday. I haven't seen them in almost three months!

e ___1___ What are you doing this weekend?

f ______ No, they're going to get a hotel room. My place is pretty small.

B Answer the questions using your own words.

1 Do you have a large extended family?

____

2 When are you going to see your family next?

____

3 When is your next family holiday?

____

2B

LANGUAGE FOCUS Discussing plans and arrangements

A Match the questions to the correct responses.

1 Are you doing anything special this weekend? ○

2 When are you going to call your parents? ○

3 What are you doing on Thursday night? ○

4 Is your roommate going to be around tonight? ○

5 Is your family coming this weekend? ○

6 How long is your cousin staying? ○

○ **a** I'm going to study for my test on Friday.

○ **b** A couple of days.

○ **c** No, he's not. He's going back home.

○ **d** I'm going to a concert on Sunday.

○ **e** Yes, they are.

○ **f** Later tonight.

B Find and correct the mistakes in the paragraph.

When I get off work today, I'm gone to the library to borrow a book. My book club going to discuss *Wuthering Heights*, a novel by Emily Bronte. We decided to read a classic this month. Next month we think of reading *The Da Vinci Code*.

I like this book club because the group tries to cover different genres each month. The following month is Susie's turn to choose a genre. I bet she's go choose science fiction, like she always does. It's not really my cup of tea. I prefer the classics!

C ▶ 2.2 Listen. Complete Maggie's weekend planner using information from the conversation.

Friday	**7.00 p.m.:** meet Beth at [1] ________________
Saturday	**12.00 p.m.:** meet [2] ________________ at train station **1.00 p.m.:** have lunch and go shopping **10.00 p.m.:** go to [3] ________________
Sunday	**2.00 p.m.:** [4] ________________ leaving **3.00 p.m.:** meet Todd at [5] ________________

LISTENING FOCUS Reduction of *going to* and *want to*

A ▶ 2.3 Notice how *going to* is reduced to "gonna" and *want to* to "wanna." Listen and repeat what you hear.

A: Are you going to go out?

B: No, I'm going to stay in.

A: Do you want to order a pizza?

B: No, I don't want to eat a heavy meal.

B ▶ 2.4 Listen. Complete the conversation.

A: What [1] ________________ you [2] ________________ do tonight?

B: Um … I'm not sure.

A: Well, [3] ________________ you [4] ________________ play video games?

B: No, not really. I don't [5] ________________ stay in. I really [6] ________________ go out.

C ▶ 2.5 Listen. Circle the best response.

1 **a** I'm going to take a nap. **b** I'm going to go to the movie theater.

2 **a** Yes, he does. **b** Yes, he is.

3 **a** I think I'll pass all my exams. **b** I want to travel to Europe.

4 **a** Yes, I am. **b** No, I don't.

2C

READING

Read the passage and answer the questions.

The Genographic Project has made discoveries about how humans populated the Earth.

1 National Geographic's Genographic Project wants to tell the greatest story ever told: how humans spread out from Africa tens of thousands of years ago to populate the planet. The team behind the project aims to show a complete map of early human history. To do this, scientists in eleven centers around the world collected DNA from local communities. Then they used computers to look for patterns in the DNA to better understand our shared genetic roots.

2 Ten years after the project started, scientists have a much better idea of when parts of the world were populated. But many questions remain. How many migrations out of Africa were there? How did the great empires of history, such as the Persians or the Mongols, leave their genetic marks on our DNA? What can our genes tell us about the origins of languages? And if we all originally came from the same place, why do we look so different? These are just some of the important questions the Genographic Project wants answers to.

3 The general public is playing an important role in the project. They can participate by simply providing DNA for testing. The results are going to allow people to trace the paths their early ancestors followed and help them find their own place on the human family tree. So far, around 800,000 people from 140 countries have participated in the project. But it's far from over, as scientists hope to learn the answers to their unanswered questions.

A Match each paragraph to its main topic. One topic is extra.

1 Paragraph 1 o	o **a** questions the project wants answers to
2 Paragraph 2 o	o **b** why some people don't get involved
3 Paragraph 3 o	o **c** the aims of the project
	o **d** the role of the general public

B Circle the best answer.

1 What is the main aim of the Genographic Project?

a to use people's DNA to find the single common ancestor we share

b to better understand how and when people populated the Earth

c to use the data from the DNA tests for research in fighting diseases

2 Which of these is **not** something scientists still want answers to?

a Which continent did our early ancestors first spread out from?

b What can our DNA tell us about how language first developed?

c If we came from the same place, why don't we look more similar?

LISTENING

A ▶ **2.6** Listen. Circle the best title for the talk.

a How to Participate in the Genographic Project

b What I Learned from the Genographic Project

c Recent Discoveries from the Genographic Project

B ▶ **2.6** Listen again. Circle the correct words to complete the sentences.

1 To participate in the Genographic Project, you should first (**visit a lab** / **buy a kit**).

2 To get a DNA sample, you (**spit into a tube** / **give a blood sample**).

3 The speaker refers to Neanderthals as our (**ancestors** / **cousins**).

4 Neanderthals split from humans (**500,000** / **60,000**) years ago.

5 The last Neanderthals lived in (**Africa** / **Europe and Asia**).

C **CRITICAL THINKING** Look back at the four questions in Paragraph 2 of the reading passage. Which question do you think is the most important one to answer? Why?

____

____

VOCABULARY BUILDING

A Complete the sentences using the words in the box.

adopted	ancestors	trace	wealth	with ease

1 If you want to __________ your family tree, start by talking to your grandparents.

2 My grandparents were very rich, but they lost all their __________ during the Great Depression.

3 Some __________ children use genealogy websites to search for their birth parents.

4 The clerk at the courthouse found my great-grandparents' marriage license __________.

5 My grandmother told me her __________ moved here from Central Europe in the 1790s.

B Read the passage. Then complete each sentence using the correct form of the words in **bold**.

What influences the **gender** of a baby? Researchers looked back over multiple **generations** of families and found that men with more brothers fathered more boys, while men with more sisters fathered more girls. Perhaps this is another reason to take an interest in **genealogy**.

1 ______________ refers to all the people born and living at about the same time.

2 ______________ is the study of family history.

3 ______________ identifies if a person is male or female.

TEDTALKS

2D

TED PLAYLIST

Human evolution is the process that led to the emergence of modern humans.

A FAMILY TREE FOR HUMANITY

Geneticist Spencer Wells studies how humanity has become so diverse. He knows that all humans share some common bits of DNA, passed down to us from our African ancestors. In this talk, he talks about how the Genographic Project will use this shared DNA to figure out how we are truly connected.

THE SEARCH FOR HUMANITY'S ROOTS

Zeresenay Alemseged digs in Africa's Ethiopian desert looking for early signs of humanity. His most exciting find is the 3.3-million-year-old skeleton of Selam, a young girl. This is the oldest skeleton of a child ever found. He talks about finding Selam and how Africa holds the clues to our human history.

A DIG FOR HUMANITY'S ORIGINS

Louise Leakey grew up in Africa and is a third generation archeologist in her family. Her grandparents were famous archeologists Louis and Mary Leakey. In this talk, she asks, "Who are we?" The question takes her back to East Africa's Rift Valley, where she digs for the origins of humankind.

A Circle the best title for the playlist.

a New Archeology Findings **b** Digging Through the Generations **c** Our shared African Past

B Which speaker most likely said the following quotes? Write **SW** (Spencer Wells), **ZA** (Zeresenay Alemseged), or **LL** (Louise Leakey).

1 "She belongs to the species known as *Australopithecus afarensis*. You don't need to remember that." ________

2 "I was very lucky to have been brought up in Kenya, essentially accompanying my parents to Lake Turkana in search of human remains." ________

3 "We were able to tell that she belonged to the human family tree because the legs, the foot, and some features clearly showed that she walked upright …" ________

4 "You can actually submit those results to the database, and tell us a little about your genealogical background, have the data analyzed as part of the scientific effort." ________

C Match each word in red to its definition.

1 humanity ○	○ **a** the point or place where something begins
2 origin ○	○ **b** the bones that support a body
3 skeleton ○	○ **c** the human family

D Decide which talk you most want to watch. Watch it online at www.ted.com.

2E

WRITING An invitation

A Read the sample email inviting family members to a future holiday event.

Write an email. Start by naming the family member(s) you want to invite to your home.

Hi, Maria and Jason!

Say what holiday you are inviting your family to.

I hope you're both well. I am writing because I want to invite you to my place for New Year's this year. I hope you don't already have plans because I'm planning something very special. I'm going to cook a large traditional meal to welcome the New Year, and I really want some of my family to be there too.

Remember to describe future plans and use some new words from this unit.

It's a great time to be here because the weather is nice, and there is a lot happening in the city. There's going to be a parade on New Year's Day that's a lot of fun. The holiday is on a Wednesday, so why don't you stay for the whole week? I have plenty of room. Please let me know soon if you can make it.

Say how long you would like your family to stay.

Sincerely,
George

B Write an email to invite some relatives to your family reunion. Answer the questions to plan your email.

1 What family member(s) do you want to invite to your home?

2 What holiday are you inviting them to?

3 What events do you have planned?

4 How long would you like them to stay with you?

C Now write your email. Then complete the checklist below.

- ☐ Did you use correct spelling and punctuation?
- ☐ Did you use some new words from this unit?
- ☐ Did you talk about future plans correctly?
- ☐ Did you say why you want your family to come?

3 Global Stories

3A

VOCABULARY Genres of fiction

A Circle the correct genres to complete the sentences.

1 The best (**thrillers** / **romance novels**) are often made into action movies.

2 I don't like reading (**horror stories** / **fairy tales**) at night because they're too scary.

3 I enjoy stories that are set in the past, so I read a lot of (**horror stories** / **historical fiction**).

4 (**Sci-fi** / **Fantasy**) novels are usually set in the future.

5 In (**graphic novels** / **romance novels**), the theme is generally love or relationships.

B Complete the passage using the genres in the box.

fan fiction	fairy tales	graphic novels	sci-fi novels

When I was young, I loved to read stories about princes and princesses and magical creatures. There's often a lesson to be learned at the end of these [1]__________________. As a teenager, I started reading a lot of [2]__________________ because I was so interested in things like aliens and spaceships.

Now that I'm an adult, my reading tastes have changed. The books I read are in comic-book form, but [3]__________________ are actually written for adults, and most have serious literary themes. I also like reading [4]__________________, where people write new stories based on the characters from popular novels, TV shows, and movies.

LISTENING My favorite book

▶ 3.1 Listen. Circle the correct answer.

1 Which novel has been adapted for television?

a *Wolf Hall* b *The Wind-Up Bird Chronicle*

2 What can we infer about *Wolf Hall*?

a It's historical fiction. b It's a romance novel.

3 What can we infer about *The Wind-Up Bird Chronicle*?

a The characters are like the ones in *Wolf Hall*. b Not everyone agrees on which genre it is.

4 What do both authors have in common?

a Their books were adapted for television. b They have unique writing styles.

COMMUNICATION Talking about books

A Read the conversation. Replace the words in **bold** using the most suitable words in the box.

absolutely	odd	romance novel	sci-fi story	travels forward in time

A: Have you read *The Time Traveler's Wife* by Audrey Niffenegger?

B: No, I don't think so. Is it a **story set in the future**? [1] ______________

A: Well, yeah but it's also a **love story**. It's about this woman whose husband has a rare medical condition, and he **goes into the future**. He also goes back to the past. [2] ______________ [3] ______________

B: It sounds **strange**—but kind of interesting. Would you recommend it? [4] ______________

A: **Definitely**. I can lend it to you when I finish it. [5] ______________

B Answer the questions using your own words.

1 What's your favorite book?

____.

2 What is it about?

____.

3 Why would you recommend it?

____.

3B

LANGUAGE FOCUS Describing stories

A Unscramble the words. There is one extra word in each sentence.

1 a hero / ~~Batman~~ / who / the public / where / protects / is /

Batman ____.

2 novel / who / a bus / ~~This~~ / is about / crashes / that /

This ____.

3 who / the school / is / Harry Potter / a student / ~~Hogwarts~~ / is / where

Hogwarts ____.

B Circle the correct words to complete the paragraph.

Andrés Neuman grew up in Buenos Aires, Argentina, [1](**that** / **where**) he was born in 1977. He has written novels, poetry, and short stories, including several [2](**that** / **who**) have won international awards. His award winning novel, *Traveller of the Century,* was his first to be published in English. In 2016, his novel *The Things We Don't Do* won the Best Translated Book Award. Experts [3](**where** / **who**) have praised his work include John Williams of *The New York Times*, and the Chilean novelist, Roberto Bolaño.

C ▶ **3.2** Listen to the conversation. Match the two parts of each sentence.

1 Aravind Adiga is a novelist	o	o	**a** that they are talking about.
2 India is the country	o	o	**b** who dreams of a better life.
3 *The White Tiger* is the novel	o	o	**c** who was born in 1974.
4 It's about a man	o	o	**d** where Adiga's novels are set.

LISTENING FOCUS Dropped /v/ sound in *of*

A ▶ **3.3** In spoken English, the word *of* is usually unstressed, and it is common for the *f* (pronounced /v/) to be dropped. In which sentences can you hear the /v/ sound? Listen and repeat what you hear.

A lot **of** people I know like historical novels.

Most **of** the time he reads romance novels.

None **of** Amy's friends like science fiction.

A lot **of** authors work long hours.

B ▶ **3.4** Circle the correct words to complete the information. Then listen and check your answers.

Native speakers often drop the /v/ sound in *of*. However, if the word that comes [1](**before** / **after**) *of* begins with a vowel sound, then the /v/ sound is usually [2](**pronounced** / **not pronounced**).

C ▶ **3.5** In which of the sentences below do you think you will hear the /v/ sound in *of*? Listen and check your answers.

1. A lot **of** people have started reading fan fiction.
2. I enjoy sci-fi stories, but I like thrillers best **of** all.
3. Some **of** my friends joined a book group.
4. None **of** our children likes to read.
5. There's a box **of** books on the table.
6. If you hear **of** any events, let me know.
7. I spend most **of** my money on books.
8. Most **of** the time, I read romance novels.

3C

READING

Read the passage and answer the questions.

We challenged Tony Miller, a local blogger, to read three genres of books that he doesn't normally like. These are his reviews.

★★★☆ *Anya's Ghost* by Vera Brosgol (2011)

1 My work colleague, Sang, recommended her favorite graphic novel, *Anya's Ghost*. The main character, Anya, is a Russian teenager who goes to live in America. Life at school is difficult because she doesn't have many friends. One day Anya meets Emily, a 90-year-old ghost, and everything changes. It explores identity and friendship, two themes that are important to everyone. I was surprised that I liked this novel, since I don't usually like graphic novels.

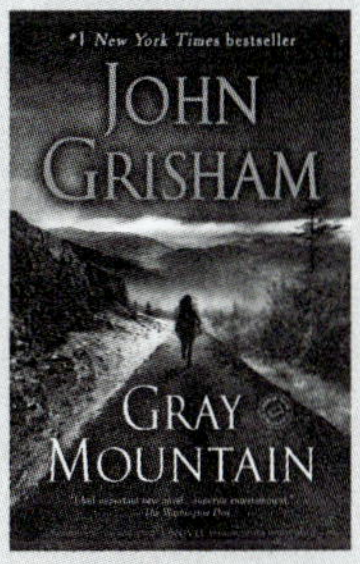

★★☆☆ *Gray Mountain* by John Grisham (2014)

2 A friend, Miguel, recommended *Gray Mountain,* a story about dishonesty in the legal profession and the damage that coal mining does to the environment. It's a revealing portrait of the struggles faced by poor people in small mining communities. It's an entertaining book with lots of suspense. Although the plot is good, this just isn't my type of novel. I'm still not a fan of thrillers.

★★★★ *Fahrenheit 451* by Ray Bradbury (1953)

3 My neighbor, Katie, knows I'm not interested in sci-fi stories, but she persuaded me to try *Fahrenheit 451*. It's set in an imagined future where books are illegal. Guy Montag is a government worker responsible for burning all books, but he begins to question the idea that they are dangerous. I loved this novel! It gives us a fascinating glimpse into a strange world where reading is against the law. I thought it was marvelous!

A Circle the correct words to complete the summary.

The article features three book reviews. [1](**An author** / **A blogger**) wrote the reviews, and each book is of a different [2](**genre** / **price**). He follows the same pattern in every review. First, he tells us the [3](**theme** / **title**), and who recommended the book to him. Then he describes the novel's [4](**plot** / **style**) and characters. He ends by telling us whether or not he enjoyed the book.

B Circle the correct answers.

1 The reviewer ________.

a didn't like these novels **b** wouldn't normally read these genres **c** liked these books

2 Which novel has a supernatural element?

a *Anya's Ghost* **b** *Gray Mountain* **c** *Fahrenheit 451*

3 Why was the reviewer surprised by the graphic novel he read?

a It had interesting themes. **b** He usually doesn't like this genre. **c** It had a lot of suspense.

4 "It's just not my type of novel" means "I ________ this kind of book."

a don't like **b** don't mind **c** love

LISTENING

A 3.6 Listen. Which word best describes how the speaker feels about the review?

a disappointed **b** impressed **c** unhappy

B 3.6 Listen again. Circle **T** for true, **F** for false, or **NG** for not given.

1 The speaker is someone who reads a lot.	**T**	**F**	**NG**
2 Her favorite genre is historical fiction.	**T**	**F**	**NG**
3 She felt there wasn't enough detail about the novels in each review.	**T**	**F**	**NG**
4 She has recommended *Anya's Ghost* to others.	**T**	**F**	**NG**
5 She probably won't read *Gray Mountain*.	**T**	**F**	**NG**
6 She is curious about *Fahrenheit 451*.	**T**	**F**	**NG**

C **CRITICAL THINKING** Based on the reviews, which book would you want to read? Give a reason for your answer.

____

Reason: ______________________________________

VOCABULARY BUILDING

A Match each word to its definition.

1 ambitious	**a** making significant or important information known
2 glimpse	**b** trying something that's not easy to achieve
3 identity	**c** surprising or extraordinary
4 marvelous	**d** a brief sense of something
5 revealing	**e** the qualities that make us who we are

B Read the passage. Then match each word in **bold** to its definition.

It's a novel that enjoyed **enormous** popularity some years ago. **Numerous** authors have tried to copy its style, but none have succeeded. It tells the **humorous** story of an **adventurous** grandmother who decides to walk from Chicago to New York. In spite of **horrendous** weather conditions, she achieves her goal ... with the help of some kind strangers.

1 adventurous	**a** very large in size or amount
2 enormous	**b** many; a lot of
3 horrendous	**c** funny and amusing
4 humorous	**d** daring; not afraid of danger
5 numerous	**e** very unpleasant or shocking

3D

TED PLAYLIST

TEDTALKS

Reading engages the imagination and opens up a whole new world for children.

FINDING THE STORY INSIDE THE PAINTING

When Tracy Chevalier looks at paintings, she imagines the stories behind them: How did the painter meet his model? What would explain that look in her eye? Why is that man blushing? She shares three stories inspired by portraits, including the one that led to her best-selling novel, *Girl With a Pearl Earring*.

HOW BOOKS CAN OPEN YOUR MIND

No one took Lisa Bu's childhood dreams seriously, so she found happiness in books instead. When she moved from China to the United States to go to graduate school, she invented new ways of reading. She discovered that books empower us, even when our dreams don't come true.

WHAT FEAR CAN TEACH US

Writer Karen Thompson Walker makes the link between fear and imagination. Through storytelling, she illustrates how books and imagination connect. Like stories, fears have a plot, characters, and suspense. Walker shows how reading may help us understand our fears.

A Circle the best title for the playlist.

a Inspiring Stories **b** Popular Children's Books **c** Overcoming the Fear of Reading

B Match each quote to the correct speaker.

1 "So if we think of our fears as more than just fears but as stories, we should think of ourselves as the authors of those stories." o

2 "What made me stop in my tracks about her to begin with was just the gorgeous colors he uses and the light falling on her face." o

3 "Books have given me a magic portal [or *gate*] to connect with people of the past and the present. I know I'll never feel lonely or powerless again." o

o **a** Tracy Chevalier

o **b** Lisa Bu

o **c** Karen Thompson Walker

C Circle the correct words to complete the sentences.

1 A portrait is a painting of (**an individual** / **scenery**).

2 If you do things to empower yourself, it means you're making yourself (**less confident** / **more confident**).

3 If you illustrate something, it means you explain it in a way that makes it (**harder** / **easier**) to understand.

D Decide which talk you most want to watch. Watch it online at www.ted.com.

3E

WRITING A book recommendation

A Read the sample book review.

Begin by stating the title and the author.

I recently read *Longbourn* by the British author, Jo Baker. It's based on the famous 19th-century novel, *Pride and Prejudice*, by Jane Austen. But, in *Longbourn*, Jo Baker invents the story of the servants who work for the Bennet family in *Pride and Prejudice*.

Provide some general information about the novel.

Describe the genre, setting, characters, and plot.

The genre is historical fiction, but you could also say it's a romance novel. The story is set in England. The main characters are two servants, Sarah and James, who fall in love. War and other problems keep them apart, but a change in circumstances brings them together. I enjoyed the suspense! I highly recommend this marvelous book to those who enjoy this genre.

Mention something you liked or didn't like about the book and finish by saying whether you recommend the book.

B Think about a book you recently read. It can be a book you liked or didn't like. Answer the questions to plan your review.

1 What is the title, and who is the author?

2 Can you briefly describe the genre, setting, characters, and plot?

3 Can you say something that you liked or didn't like about the book?

4 Would you recommend it to others?

C Now write your review. Then complete the checklist below.

☐ Did you use correct spelling and punctuation?

☐ Did you provide the title, author, genre, setting, characters, and plot?

☐ Did you describe something you liked or didn't like about the book?

☐ Did you say whether or not you would recommend it?

4 Music

4A

VOCABULARY Music

Complete the puzzle using the words in the box. One is extra.

country	rhythmic	dark	hip-hop
energized	romantic	melancholic	nostalgic

Across

2 music that makes you think of love
4 music that reminds you of the past
7 music that has a regular repeated sound

Down

1 feeling lively and upbeat
3 music that makes you feel moody or sad
5 music that is originally from the southern and western United States
6 music that is gloomy and negative

LISTENING Music preferences

A 4.1 Listen. What topic is each person discussing? Number the topics in the order you hear them.

a ___ a recent concert **b** ___ a song **c** ___ music lessons

B 4.1 Listen again. Answer the questions.

1 Why doesn't Linda like the song?

______

2 How does Mark feel about his neighbor's taste in music?

______

3 How did Susan feel at the concert?

______

COMMUNICATION Talking about music

A Circle the correct words to complete the sentences.

1 **A:** Can you play any country music songs?

B: Yeah, I know (**a few** / **a little**).

2 **A:** What are you listening to?

B: Oh, it's a (**song** / **music**) by Beyoncé.

3 **A:** Do you ever listen to heavy metal music?

B: No, never. I find it too (**loud** / **soft**). I can't hear myself think!

4 **A:** Are there any hip-hop songs on this playlist?

B: Yeah, there are (**some** / **no**) old songs but nothing new.

B Complete the conversation using your own words.

A: Thanks for participating in this short survey. So what kind of music do you like?

B: Oh, I like a lot, but my favorites are [1]________________ and [2]________________.

A: Really? Do you have any pop music on your phone?

B: [3]______________________________.

A: So what is your favorite song?

B: It's [4]________________ by [5]________________.

A: This was most helpful. Thank you for your time.

4B

LANGUAGE FOCUS Discussing types of music

A Circle the correct words to complete the information.

Composers of electronic music usually use just a [1](**few** / **little**) instruments to make music, such as drum machines, keyboards, and synthesizers. [2](**Little** / **A lot of**) prerecorded sounds are used in [3](**much** / **many**) of their performances.

[4](**Many** / **Much**) people confuse electronic music with techno, but they are not the same. Techno is just one type of electronic music. In fact there are [5](**many** / **much**) others.

B Rewrite each sentence so that it has the same meaning. Change the words in **bold**.

1 I **have no** country music on my phone.

____.

2 Do you have **much** music on your laptop?

____?

3 **Not many** people like this song.

____.

C ▶ 4.2 Listen. Complete the sentences using information from the conversation.

1 The man thinks there's ____________ hip-hop.

2 The woman doesn't have ____________ heavy metal.

3 The man asks how ____________ electronic music is on the playlist.

4 The woman says she has ____________ electronic music on her playlist.

LISTENING FOCUS Stress patterns

A ▶ 4.3 Listen and notice the different stress patterns in these two- and three-syllable words.

O o	o O	O o o	o O o
mu / sic	**re / laxed**	**au / di / ence**	**ro / man / tic**

B ▶ 4.4 Listen and underline the stressed syllable in each word.

1 attitude
2 nostalgic
3 passion
4 rhythmic
5 reduce
6 energized
7 keyboard
8 performer

C ▶ 4.5 Write the words in the correct columns. Then listen and check your answers.

~~composer~~ **spooky** **musical** **instrument**
gentle **musician** **effect** **classical**

O o	o O	O o o	o O o
			composer

4C

READING

Read the passage and answer the questions below.

1 People have known for a long time that music affects our motivation to exercise. But only in the past ten years have researchers understood why exercise and music go so well together.

2 Music distracts the brain during exercise. When you begin to feel tired or sore, your brain tells you to stop or slow down. Music competes with this information and can help you overcome the impulse to take a break. Listening to music has other effects, too. It lifts your mood. It increases endurance. It may even make your body more efficient. Music can help you swim faster, run farther, and pedal longer without even realizing it. It is so powerful that some organizations ban music during marathons so that no runner gets a competitive edge.

Studies have shown that music eases the pain of working out.

3 Different types of music have different tempos—or the speed at which music is played. For example, jazz is played at about 110 beats per minute (bpm), hip-hop and pop at 110–140 bpm, and techno at 120–160 bpm. To get the maximum benefit, match the music to the type of exercise you are doing. When walking at a moderate speed, most people favor music around 125 bpm. When running, they prefer music at 160 bpm.

4 But choosing the most effective music is not as simple as filling up your phone with fast songs. For many people, how much they identify with the singer's emotional state determines how motivated they feel to keep moving. In short, if you find a song gets you moving, play it!

A What is the passage mainly about?

a the effect of music on exercise **b** types of music and their tempos **c** the best music to play at the gym

B Circle the best answer.

1 What is **not** given as a reason why music helps with exercise?
- **a** It relaxes your muscles.
- **b** It increases endurance.
- **c** It distracts the brain from feeling tired.

2 What would be the best music choice if you wanted to go for a run?

a hip-hop **b** techno **c** pop

3 Which of these does the author suggest you think about when choosing a song to exercise to?

a how long it is **b** how loud you play it **c** how it makes you feel

LISTENING

A ▶ **4.6** Listen. What type of talk is it?

a an advertisement **b** a lecture **c** a review

B ▶ **4.6** Listen again. Circle the best answer.

1 The product has GPS and the ability to monitor your ________.

a heart rate **b** fat burn

2 Which of these will cause the "coach" to tell a person to slow down?

a playing a fast song **b** increased heart rate

3 Which feature did the speaker **not** like?

a the coach's voice is too loud **b** only chooses music from speaker's collection

C **CRITICAL THINKING** Circle the feature you think would most improve the smart trainer. Give a reason for your answer.

a calculate calories burnt **c** match song's tempo to exercise

b play songs faster or slower **d** measure heart rate accurately

Reason: ____

VOCABULARY BUILDING

A Complete the sentences using the words in the box.

chemical	effect	registers	research	turn on

1 To hear what music is popular right now, just ________ the radio.

2 Scientists are making huge advances in brain ________.

3 Your brain ________ that you are full 20 minutes after eating.

4 Love songs can have a powerful ________ on people.

5 Serotonin is a(n) ________ found in several parts of the body, including the brain.

B Read the passage. Then complete the sentences below using the phrases in **bold**.

How do you feel when you listen to Pharrell Williams's "Happy"? If you're like millions of others, you feel … happy. Maybe you even **turn up** the song and sing along when you hear it. The hit single was even **turned into** a children's book. But the 2015 hit is not the happiest song of all time. According to *Billboard* magazine, it **turns out** that it's The Turtles' 1967 song "Happy Together."

1 It ________ that musicians make great language learners.

2 ________ the music if you can't hear it.

3 The shy student has ________ a major singing star.

TEDTALKS

4D

TED PLAYLIST

Ji-Hae Park playing her violin for commuters at the Chabacano Station, Mexico

For guitarist Teitur, singing is about giving away a piece of yourself to others. "If your intentions are to impress people or to get the big applause at the end," he says, "then you are taking, not giving." Listen as he performs on stage, offering two songs about love, distance, and home.

In her quest to become a world-famous violinist, Ji-Hae Park fell into severe depression. Only music was able to lift her out of the darkness—showing her that her goal need not be to play majestic halls but instead to bring the wonder of the instrument to as many people as possible.

Are you ready to dance in your seat? Drummer Clayton Cameron breaks down different genres of music—from R&B to Latin to pop—by their beats. This is a talk that proves hip-hop and jazz aren't cooler than math—they actually rely on it.

A Match each talk title to the correct speaker.

1 A-rhythm-etic. The Math Behind the Beats o — o **a** Teitur
2 Home is a Song I've Always Remembered o — o **b** Ji-Hae Park
3 The Violin—and My Dark Night of the Soul o — o **c** Clayton Cameron

B Circle the best answer.

1 Which speaker is also a singer?
a Teitur **b** Ji-Hae Park **c** Clayton Cameron

2 What is true about Ji-Hae Park?
a She likes to play in the dark.
b Music got her out of her depression.
c Her main goal is to play world-famous music halls.

3 What does Clayton Cameron want to achieve in his talk?
a He wants to show the relationship between math and music.
b He wants to demonstrate how fun it is to dance in your seat.
c He wants to show how each music genre uses unique instruments.

C Complete the sentences using the words in red.

1 A ____________________ is a long, difficult search for something.
2 If you ____________________ someone, the person admires and respects you.
3 When you ____________________ something, you make it easier to understand.

D Decide which talk you most want to watch. Watch it online at www.ted.com.

4E

WRITING A favorite song

A Read the sample passage about a song from someone's childhood.

Start by naming the song and artist, and saying where or when you first heard it.	When I was 11 or 12 years old, I remember hearing the song "Stronger" by Kanye West for the first time. I remember I was at the mall and my friend played it for me. I didn't really know who Kanye West was at the time. I mostly listened to pop music, but then I started to listen to hip-hop more and more.	Describe your musical tastes at that time and other details you remember.
Describe what you thought of the song. Describe why you liked it and how it made you feel.	I thought it was a really cool song. I downloaded it and later saw the video online. I even learned the lyrics. I was going through a difficult time at school then, and this song made me feel strong and confident. I sometimes hear the song, and it still gives me the same feelings. But I think my musical taste has changed. I'm more into electronic and techno these days.	Say what you think of the song now and describe your musical tastes today. Remember to use words from this unit.

B Write about your favorite song from your childhood. Answer the questions to plan your passage.

1 What is the name of the song? Who is it by?

2 How old were you when you first heard the song?

3 How did the song make you feel?

4 What do you think of the song now? Are your musical tastes different now?

C Now write your passage. Then complete the checklist below.

- ☐ Did you use correct spelling and punctuation?
- ☐ Did you describe why you bought or downloaded the song?
- ☐ Did you use some new words from this unit?
- ☐ Did you describe how the song affected you?

5 Good Design

5A

VOCABULARY Design elements

A Match each word to its definition.

1 color		**a** the difference between unlike or opposite qualities
2 contrast		**b** the forms that things take (for example, square or triangular)
3 lines		**c** the way something feels when you touch it
4 shapes		**d** long thin marks that are drawn or painted on a surface
5 sizes		**e** how big or small things are
6 texture		**f** a quality (such as red, blue, or green) that you see when you look at something

B Circle the correct words to complete the paragraph.

Everyone expected Rosie to wear bright colors, but instead she chose a [1](**subtle** / **vibrant**) blue dress with a very big orange belt—the belt was [2](**huge** / **tiny**)! The contrast between these two colors was very [3](**subtle** / **dramatic**). The texture of the fabric was really soft and [4](**smooth** / **rough**). Across the shoulders at the top of the dress there were small, silver circles. Their [5](**round** / **square**) shape matched her necklace, and their [6](**square** / **curved**) lines were the same blue as her eyes. Beautiful!

LISTENING A designer's advice

A ▶ 5.1 Listen. Circle the best answer.

1 How does the woman feel about buying the car?

a she's not sure **b** she's not interested

2 What is her friend's attitude about the car?

a he's bored **b** he's excited

3 Is she going to buy the car?

a yes **b** maybe

B ▶ 5.1 Listen again. Complete the notes using information from the conversation.

1 wants to buy: ___a new car___

2 color she wants: ________

3 she likes: the ________ between the colors

4 also likes: the ________ of the seats

5 doesn't like: the ________ lines at the front

COMMUNICATION Talking about design

A Circle the best response.

1 Do you like this coat?

a She doesn't like it. **b** Not really.

2 I don't like the shape at all.

a But it's so unique! **b** It's $50.

3 What do you think of this one?

a The texture is too rough. **b** You're most welcome.

4 I really like the colors.

a The price is reasonable. **b** Yeah, the contrast is interesting.

B Look at the picture. Answer the questions using your own words.

1 Do you like the chair in the photo?

____.

2 What do you like about it?

____.

3 What do you not like about it?

____.

5B

LANGUAGE FOCUS Discussing elements of design

A Circle the correct words to complete the sentences.

1 The circle is (**in** / **on**) front of the square.

2 There's a symbol (**at** / **inside**) the circle.

3 This sign is (**in** / **at**) the shape of a triangle.

4 The motto is (**in** / **at**) the top of the crest.

B Look at the signs. Complete the descriptions.

1 There is a bicycle ____________________ the circle.

2 There are arrows ____________________ the left and the right.

3 There is a red border ____________________ the sign.

4 The dot is ____________________ the bottom of the sign.

C 5.2 Look at the coat of arms. Complete the description with the correct prepositions of place. Then listen and check your answers.

A shield is [1](**in the middle** / **on the right**) of the coat of arms. There is a black border [2](**below** / **around**) the shield. A large key and an arrow are crossed in the center of the shield. The bottom of the arrow is [3](**on the left** / **on the right**) and the bottom of the key is on the right. [4](**Around** / **Above**) the shield, there is a crown. There is a lion to the left of the shield, and another one [5](**to the left** / **to the right**) of it. There is a banner [6](**above** / **below**) the shield.

LISTENING FOCUS Dropped /d/ and /t/

A 5.3 Read the sentences, and pay attention to the letters in red. The /d/ and /t/ sounds are often dropped (not pronounced) when they are followed by another consonant sound. They are not dropped, however, when they are followed by a vowel sound. Listen and repeat what you hear.

The contrast **an~~d~~ colors** make it an exciting design.

It **mus~~t~~ be** difficult to work with him.

It **rained all** afternoon.

The **patient asked** for another pillow.

B 5.4 Listen to the conversation. Draw a line through each /d/ or /t/ in red that is dropped.

A: Kim, sorry, I can't [1]find the design plans.

B: I think Bob [2]might be using them.

A: Right. Can you ask him to [3]send them to me, please?

B: Oh, … I [4]just found them, but the latest changes haven't been made yet.

A: Great! Can you add the changes and email them to me [5]right away?

B: Sorry, I'm [6]just about to go into a meeting.

A: That's OK. It can [7]wait until the afternoon.

B: Sure, that [8]should be no problem.

A: Great. As long as I have them by the [9]end of the day.

B: No problem. You can [10]depend on me!

C 5.5 Listen. Complete the sentences using the words you hear.

1 The ______________________ of my country's flag is blue.

2 I really like the ______________________ stripes on this flag.

3 This is the ______________________ flag I've ever seen.

4 It's only the ______________________ I've seen this flag.

5C

READING

Read the passage and answer the questions below.

The Olympic flag is symbolic in showing that the games are intended for all nations to come together and compete in unity.

1 The Olympic Games were first held in Greece nearly three thousand years ago. They were very popular for over a thousand years before stopping in 393 A.D. They started again in 1896 in Athens, thanks to a bold idea from a Frenchman named Pierre de Coubertin.

2 In 1913, de Coubertin designed the Olympic flag. He showed it for the first time in 1914 at a meeting of the International Olympic Committee (IOC) in Paris. However, the flag was not used at the games until the 1920 Olympics in Antwerp.

3 Its design is simple. The idea comes from a stone discovered at Delphi, the ancient site of the original games. The flag is white with five connecting circles in the center, representing the five continents that take part in the Olympics. The international symbolism of these linked circles is a powerful one. Each circle is a different color—blue, yellow, black, green, and red. These represent the colors found in the national flag of every participating country. The white background symbolizes peace.

4 At every opening ceremony, athletes from the host country carry in the Olympic flag and take an oath, or promise, to honor the games and play by the rules. The flag and its five-ring logo are protected in most countries and may only be used for official Olympic purposes. The Olympic flag is one of the world's most recognized flags, because it is something that represents so many of us.

A According to the passage, what is true about the Olympic flag?

a The flag was first used at the 1896 Olympics in Athens.

b No one has permission to use the flag unless it's for official Olympic business.

c The connecting circles represent the five countries that participate in the games.

B Match each paragraph to the correct heading. One heading is extra.

1 Paragraph 1 ○	○	**a** What does the flag symbolize?
2 Paragraph 2 ○	○	**b** How is the flag used?
3 Paragraph 3 ○	○	**c** What is the history of the Olympics?
4 Paragraph 4 ○	○	**d** How often are the games held?
	○	**e** When was the flag first used?

LISTENING

A ▶ **5.6** Listen. What are the speakers talking about?

a what the Olympic flag represents **b** the history of the Olympic games **c** who designed the Olympic flag

B ▶ **5.6** Listen again. Circle the best answer.

1 How does the man feel about the Olympic flag?

a He sounds pretty excited about it. **b** He hasn't thought about it very much.

2 What is the woman's attitude toward the Olympic Games?

a She doesn't understand sports. **b** She's not a sports fan at all.

3 The man's favorite thing about the flag is that it represents ______.

a the world's oldest sporting event **b** something positive in the world

4 Does the woman change her opinion in the end?

a Yes, she does. **b** No, she doesn't.

C **CRITICAL THINKING** Is your own opinion of the Olympic flag more like the man's or the woman's? Give a reason for your answer.

____

Reason: ____

VOCABULARY BUILDING

A Complete the sentences using the words in the box.

bold	distinct	popular	symbolism	tool

1 As a graphic designer, my most important ______________ is my laptop.

2 The design on the artifact was filled with religious ______________.

3 Their approach to design was very ______________. They were not afraid to try weird ideas.

4 Everyone voted on their favorite design, and this was the most ______________ one.

5 The problem with this logo is that it's not ______________ enough. It's just too similar to the others.

B Complete the sentences using the correct form of the words in **bold**.

verb ends in *-ize*	noun ends in *-ism*
to point out the problems or faults in someone or something: **criticize**	**criticism**
to serve as or be a symbol of: **symbolize**	**symbolism**

People [1]______________ ugly logo designs, but my main [2]______________ is when logos are not bold or distinct enough. Do something unique. Use [3]______________ to create something that [4]______________ what you do, what you stand for, and what you want people to know about you.

5D TED PLAYLIST

Evolution of *The New York Times* over the years

TEDTALKS

THE FIRST SECRET OF DESIGN IS ... NOTICING

Product designer Tony Fadell discusses original approaches to good design. He offers some useful encouragement to designers, asking them to pay close attention to details, the way children do. He believes when we really notice things, we find ways to make them better by asking the right questions.

GREAT DESIGN IS SERIOUS, NOT SOLEMN

Designer Paula Scher shares some interesting experiences from over 30 years working in the profession. She uses the terms *serious* or *solemn,* suggesting that *solemn* work is boring. But her best designs are created when she does *serious* work, which she often calls *serious play*.

CAN DESIGN SAVE NEWSPAPERS?

Jacek Utko was an architect who started designing newspapers in Eastern Europe at a time when most people had already stopped buying them. He got rid of the old look and improved the product to give the reader a better experience. His designs dramatically increased newspaper sales.

A Which is the best title for the playlist?

- **a** How to Create Designs that Win Big Awards
- **b** Designers and the Common Mistakes They Make
- **c** What We Can Learn from Successful Designers

B Circle the best answers.

1 Why does Tony Fadell encourage designers to think like children?
- **a** Children have a lot of fun and don't take anything seriously.
- **b** Children have the ability to see things in a fresh new way.

2 What can we infer about Paula Scher's view of solemn designs?
- **a** They're too formal and often not very creative.
- **b** She doesn't have much experience with them.

3 Which of these is a better description of Jacek Utko's approach?
- **a** He is mainly interested in increasing newspaper sales.
- **b** He really thinks about the customers and wants them to enjoy reading the paper.

C Complete the sentences using the words in red.

1 If someone ________________ you advice, you can choose to follow or ignore it.

2 Jacek Utko had a different ________________ before he became a designer.

3 We kept the best ideas and ________________ the ones that weren't working.

D Decide which talk you most want to watch. Watch it online at www.ted.com.

5E

WRITING My country's flag

A Read the sample passage about Jamaica's flag.

In the first sentence, state what flag you are describing.

I come from Jamaica, and my country's flag has a very nice design. It uses three colors: yellow, green, and black.

Next, say what colors are used in the flag.

Then, describe the design of the flag.

Two thick yellow lines meet in the center of the flag, like an *X*. At the top and bottom of the yellow *X*, there are green triangles. To the left and right of the yellow *X*, there are black triangles.

Finish by explaining what the colors of the flag represent

Each color on the flag symbolizes something unique about my country. Black represents the strength and creativity of the people. The yellow represents the natural wealth and beauty of sunlight, and green symbolizes hope and agricultural resources.

Try to use some new words from this unit.

B Describe your country's flag. Answer the questions to plan your passage.

1 What flag are you describing? What colors does it use?

2 Can you describe the flag in detail? Can you use prepositions of place to explain where each element is?

3 Can you explain what the colors represent?

C Now write your passage. Then complete the checklist below.

- ☐ Did you use correct spelling and punctuation?
- ☐ Did you state the country and describe the colors and design of the flag?
- ☐ Did you use some new words from this unit?
- ☐ Did you explain what the colors represent?

6 Inspiration

6A

VOCABULARY Sources of inspiration

A Complete the sentences using the correct form of the words in the box.

change	encourage	give	is	show	support

1 My grandparents always ______________ me to do my best.
2 Her father's discovery completely ______________ their lives. They are now famous!
3 He ______________ a role model for his younger siblings.
4 My music teacher ______________ my decision to audition for the orchestra.
5 Our parents always ______________ us great advice.
6 She ______________ them that with hard work, nothing was impossible.

B Answer the questions using your own words.

1 What is the best gift you have received? Who gave it to you?

____

2 What's your favorite book? Who wrote it?

____

3 Name someone who became famous at an early age. What made that person famous?

____

LISTENING My inspiration

A ▶ 6.1 Listen to a person talking about people who inspire her. Number the three people (**1–3**) in the order you hear them. One is extra.

a _____ a teacher
b _____ a coworker
c _____ a friend
d _____ a neighbor

B ▶ 6.1 Listen again. How did each of them inspire the speaker? Complete the sentences.

1 Kevin said to do ______________ work even though the speaker doesn't think she has ______________.
2 Katie asked the speaker to join her in starting a ______________ selling ______________ cakes.
3 George told her to keep ______________ because he thought she had a lot of ______________.

COMMUNICATION Talking about an inspirational person

A Circle the correct words to complete the conversations.

1 **A:** I had a great teacher in high school. She really inspired me.
B: Did she (**give** / **ask**) you any good advice?
A: Yeah, she did. She (**said** / **told**) me to study hard and never give up.

2 **A:** My grandfather (**asked** / **gave**) me some great advice a few months ago.
B: Oh yeah? What was it?
A: Well, I really like fashion. He (**said** / **asked**) that I should start a blog. So I did!

3 **A:** I think Kate Middleton is an (**encouragement** / **inspiration**) to a lot of people.
B: Why is that?
A: She once (**said** / **told**) that she wanted to be a good mother. And I think she is.

B Answer the questions using your own words.

1 Which of your teachers did you find inspiring?

____

2 Did this teacher give you any advice? If so, what did he or she say?

____

3 Did you follow the advice that was given to you? How did it change your life?

____

6B

LANGUAGE FOCUS Discussing inspirational people

A Circle the correct word to complete the sentences.

1 My music teacher (**said** / **told**) me to practice more often.
2 My mother once (**said** / **told**) that I should take a year off before I started college.
3 Alice's friends (**said** / **told**) that they liked her drawings.
4 My parents (**said** / **told**) me to always look adults in the eye.
5 My father (**said** / **told**) that he really admired Bill Gates.
6 Our teacher once (**said** / **told**) us not to be late anymore.

B Read the conversation. Then complete the sentences below.

Michele: Look at that painting.

Brad: Ugh, I don't like it at all.

Michele: I agree!

Brad: I prefer the first one we looked at.

Michele: Yeah, I think so too.

Michele told Brad to look at the painting.

Brad said ______________________________.

Michele said ______________________________.

Brad told ______________________________.

Michele said ______________________________.

C ▶ 6.2 Listen to a man talking about his grandmother. Circle the correct words to complete the sentences.

1 His grandmother told him (**to quit** / **not to quit**) his job.

2 She said that he should find something he (**loved** / **was good at**).

3 When he missed a goal, she (**said** / **didn't say**) that it was OK.

4 She told him to (**study** / **practice**) more.

5 She told him and his brother to (**walk** / **drive**) to the mall.

LISTENING FOCUS Pausing after commas

A ▶ 6.3 Notice how there is often a slight pause after a comma. Listen and repeat what you hear.

In 1995, J. K. Rowling completed the first Harry Potter book.

Despite their best efforts, the students performed poorly.

They had a long marriage, but it was not an easy one.

B ▶ 6.4 Add a comma to each sentence. Then listen for the pause to check your answers.

1 After she climbed Mt. Kilimanjaro she decided to run the London Marathon.

2 As a child his older brother was a great role model.

3 My Aunt Janet led a very traditional life but I found her very inspiring.

4 In 2016 athletes from all over the world competed at the Rio Olympic Games.

5 I handed in my project but I wasn't satisfied with my work.

C ▶ 6.5 Listen. Write the number of pauses you hear in each sentence.

1 ______ 2 ______ 3 ______ 4 ______

6C

READING

Read the passage and answer the questions below.

Fugees Family youth soccer team from the U.S. Refugee Program

Actions speak louder than words. Here are two examples of ordinary people doing extraordinary things and making a difference to those around them.

Easing the transition

1 The life of a refugee—someone forced to leave their own country—is never easy. They often struggle socially and have trouble fitting in. It's especially difficult for children.

2 Luma Mufleh is the coach of a soccer program for young refugees near Atlanta, in the United States. "You see kids that don't speak a word of English," says Mufleh, "and when they come here, their faces light up when they're on the field."

3 She began her program in 2004, but soon realized that the children had many needs beyond the soccer field. Her nonprofit Fugees Family now has its own school with programs designed to meet the refugees' needs. "This is one place they get to be kids again," says Mufleh. "They feel confident and happy." Mufleh and her organization have already helped more than 800 refugees from 28 countries.

Breaking the cycle

4 In the U.S. state of Virginia, for children born into the projects—government-supported low rent housing—cyclist Craig Dodson is doing something to change their lives. Since he started the nonprofit Richmond Cycling Corps in 2010, he has worked to create and coach cycling teams for children living in the projects.

5 He works with children who do bicycle training several times a week. However, the primary goal is about more than cycling. According to Dodson, it's "not about giving kids positive life experiences through bikes. Our job is to get them out of public housing."

6 Dodson does whatever he can because he knows how difficult it can be to get out of the projects. He takes the children to doctor visits, gets involved with school issues, and even deals with family problems. "We do whatever it takes," says Dodson.

A What is the passage mainly about?

a helping refugees in the United States **b** popular sports for young people **c** organizations that help people

B Use the information (**a–f**) to complete the Venn diagram.

a has a nonprofit organization

b started their project in 2010

c provides access to medical care

d works with children

e uses sports to help others

f works with people who once lived overseas

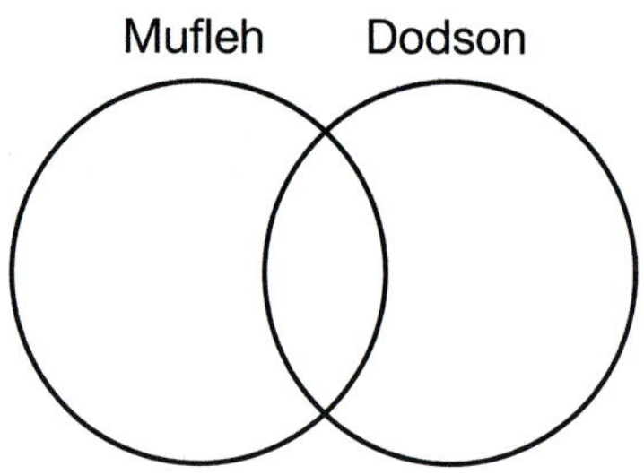

LISTENING

A ▶ 6.6 Listen to two friends discussing a blog. Circle **T** for true or **F** for false.

1	Kathy Caprino is a writer and trainer.	**T**	**F**
2	When someone asked Caprino who inspired her, she said no one.	**T**	**F**
3	Caprino found that inspiring people all have three common traits.	**T**	**F**

B ▶ 6.6 Listen again. Complete the sentences using information from the talk.

1 Inspiring people are not ________________ to set their own ________________, even when others criticize them.

2 Caprino found that the people she studied feel satisfied when they are able to ________________ and contribute to their ________________.

3 Inspiring people tell amazing ________________ because they have a ________________ way of looking at the world.

C **CRITICAL THINKING** Which of the traits identified by Kathy Caprino do you think apply to Luma Mufleh and/or Craig Dodson? Give reasons to support your opinion.

____

Reason: ____

VOCABULARY BUILDING

A Complete the information using the words in the box.

celebrate	**effort**	**fans**	**give up**

Local rock band The Sponges were on hand at Pillar Square on Sunday to [1]________________ the release of their new album. [2]________________ started lining up at noon in an attempt to get one of only 500 tickets for the event. This was part of the band's [3]________________ to raise funds for their charity, Homes for the Homeless. "We plan to raise $10,000 this year, and won't [4]________________ until we meet that goal," said lead singer Nick Branson.

B Complete the sentences using the phrases in the box.

a great deal of effort	**make an effort**	**for his efforts**

1 Sara put ________________________ into her poster presentation.

2 Joe didn't win the competition, but he was recognized ________________________.

3 I'm not very good at public speaking, but I'll ________________________.

TEDTALKS

6D

TED PLAYLIST

Children take part in the Superheroes Fun Run in Crumlin, Ireland.

EVERY KID NEEDS A CHAMPION

Rita Pierson, a teacher for 40 years, once heard a colleague say, "They don't pay me to like the kids." What was her response? "Kids don't learn from people they don't like." In this talk, she gives an inspiring call to educators to believe in their students and actually connect with them on a real, human, personal level.

KIDS, TAKE CHARGE

Kiran Bir Sethi shows how her Riverside School in India teaches kids life's most valuable lesson: "I can." The school's mission focuses on creating curious, competent future citizens. Watch her students take local issues into their own hands, lead other young people, and even educate their parents.

WHY LUNCH LADIES ARE HEROES

Children's book author Jarrett Krosoczka shares the origins of the Lunch Lady series, in which undercover school heroes serve lunch ... and justice! His new project, School Lunch Hero Day, reveals how cafeteria lunch staff provide more than food, and illustrates how powerful a thank-you can be.

A What is the theme of the playlist?

a fighting crime **b** people who inspire others **c** how children teach adults

B Circle the best answer.

1 Which speakers worked in a school?

a Kiran Bir Sethi and Jarrett Krosoczka **b** Rita Pierson and Kiran Bir Sethi **c** Rita Pierson and Jarrett Krosoczka

2 "They're feeding our children every single day, and before a child can learn, their belly needs to be full ..." Which speaker most likely said this?

a Rita Pierson **b** Kiran Bir Sethi **c** Jarrett Krosoczka

C Match each word in red to its definition.

1 champion o — o **a** done in a secret way in order to stop criminals
2 competent o — o **b** someone who defends a person or cause
3 undercover o — o **c** having the ability or skills to do something

D Decide which talk you most want to watch. Watch it online at www.ted.com.

6E

WRITING An inspiring person

A Read the sample passage about an inspiring person.

Write two paragraphs. Start by saying who the person is.

Astronaut Neil Armstrong once said, "That's one small step for man, one giant leap for mankind." Armstrong said it on July 29, 1969, after he stepped onto the moon. He was of course the first person to walk on the moon. To me, his quote means that the actual step onto the moon was simple for him, but the implications of the step were huge for all of mankind.

Explain what they did.

Remember to use new words from this unit.

It was an amazing achievement, and the whole world celebrated it. I find it inspiring because it shows that people can achieve great things if they try and don't give up. It says that nothing is impossible, and I believe there are still many challenges like this that can inspire us.

Say how their achievement makes you feel and why you find it inspiring.

B Think about a person you know that you find inspiring. Answer the questions to plan your passage.

1 Who is the person?

2 What did they do to inspire you?

3 How does their achievement make you feel?

4 Why does their achievement make you feel that way?

C Now write your passage. Then complete the checklist below.

- ☐ Did you use correct spelling and punctuation?
- ☐ Did you use some new words from this unit?
- ☐ Did you say who the person is and what they did?
- ☐ Did you say why they inspire you and how?

Audio Scripts

▶ **1.1** Monarch butterflies have amazing orange, black, and white patterns. They are mainly found in the United States and Canada, and they travel to warmer places for the winter. Some go to California, but most fly to Mexico, a distance of almost 3,000 miles. That's over 4,800 kilometers!

But the monarch butterfly is in trouble. Its population began to decline over 20 years ago. One reason for this is climate change. Hotter summers, colder winters, extreme rain, and dry weather are all contributing factors. Another reason is chemicals used in agriculture, which affect the monarchs' food source.

The monarch butterfly population has dropped by 80 percent since the early 1990s, and it is now listed as a near-threatened species. However, there is good news for the monarchs. Several conservation projects are working hard to protect them and, in 2016, a survey showed an increase in their numbers.

▶ **1.2** **A:** What is the World Wildlife Fund? **B:** The World Wildlife Fund, or WWF, is an international organization. It protects wildlife and the environment. **A:** Is the World Wildlife Fund working on projects in many countries? **B:** Yes, it is. There are WWF projects in more than 100 countries. **A:** Does the WWF get all its money from the government? **B:** No, it doesn't. It gets some funding from governments, some from corporations, and most from public donations.

▶ **1.3** **/s/:** parents, sleeps, weeks, books; **/z/:** kids, dogs, days, needs

▶ **1.4** **1.** ants; **2.** butterflies; **3.** cats; **4.** bees; **5.** pandas; **6.** tigers

▶ **1.5** **/s/:** elephants, hops; **/z/:** eyes, frogs, monkeys, penguins

▶ **1.6** I can't stop thinking about the pig-nosed turtles. Before today, I'd never even heard of them! I get so upset when I think about any creature becoming extinct. And worse, it's our fault—human beings, I mean.

I did a bit more research on them and came across the most troubling news! Pig-nosed turtles are the last surviving members of their particular family of turtles—the very last—that's awful. We have to save them. We've got to treat them with more respect!

To be honest, I really believe that we'd hear more about pig-nosed turtles in the news if they were cute, like sea lions or sea otters. Do you think they're ugly? I think they're kind of cute. Well, cute or ugly, we must protect them. Pig-nosed turtles are amazing, and I'm glad that things are improving for them at last.

▶ **2.1** I got married early last year. My wife's name is Rebecca. We have one child—a one-month-old daughter named Caitlin. We hope to have another child someday.

Right now, Rebecca, Caitlin, and I live with her parents. They have a small house but we're very comfortable. We're saving our money and hope to buy our own house someday.

Rebecca has a younger brother named Casey. He's 19 years old and in college. He's studying to be a teacher. Casey is a lot of fun to be around. I don't have any brothers, so Casey is the closest thing I have.

▶ **2.2** **A:** Hello. **B:** Hey Maggie, it's Todd. Are you busy? **A:** Oh, hi Todd. I'm just studying. But I can use the break. **B:** Cool. Listen, are you doing anything on Friday night? **A:** Um, yeah, I'm meeting Beth at the library at 7 o'clock. We're going to study for our chemistry test. **B:** Oh, OK. Well, how about Saturday? **A:** Saturday is pretty full too. My sister is coming for a visit, so I'm meeting her at the train station at noon. We're going to have lunch and then go shopping. At 10 o'clock that night I'm taking her to a nightclub. **B:** You sound really busy. **A:** But Sunday is OK. My sister is leaving at 2 o'clock in the afternoon, so I'm free after that. **B:** Great! Do you want to go to the art museum? There's a really cool modern art exhibit there. Sunday is the last day. **A:** Maybe we can meet at the museum at 3 o'clock. Does that work? **B:** Perfect! I'll see you then. Text me when you get there.

▶ **2.3** **A:** Are you going to go out? **B:** No, I'm going to stay in. **A:** Do you want to order a pizza? **B:** No, I don't want to eat a heavy meal.

▶ **2.4** **A:** What are you going to do tonight? **B:** Um. I'm not sure. **A:** Well, do you want to play video games? **B:** No, not really. I don't want to stay in. I really want to go out.

▶ **2.5** **1.** Where are you going to go later?; **2.** Does your brother want to join us?; **3.** What do you want to do after graduation?; **4.** Do you think it's going to rain?

▶ **2.6** The Genographic Project makes it very easy to participate and trace your ancestry. Here's what you need to do.

You start by purchasing a kit. Inside is a spit tube. You provide a saliva sample and mail the tube in. There's no blood test; your saliva has all the DNA that is needed.

Geneticists receive your DNA sample and run some tests. They look at thousands of genetic markers to determine who your ancestors were. There's also a test to see if you are related to our cousins, the Neanderthals.

Neanderthals split from humans around 500,000 years ago. We humans first left Africa about 60,000 years ago, when Neanderthals were still alive in Europe and Asia. It seems that our ancestors met, leaving a small genetic trace of these ancient relatives in our DNA. With the test, you can learn if you have any Neanderthal DNA.

▶ **3.1** **A:** My favorite novel? It's definitely *Wolf Hall* by Hilary Mantel. **B:** Why do you like it? **A:** It's brilliantly written. It's set in England in the period from 1500 to 1535, and is based on real people in English history. The way Hilary Mantel describes the characters is fascinating. She doesn't write like any other author I know; she has an incredible imagination. **B:** Sounds great! **A:** It really is. It's already been made into a popular TV series. So what's yours? **B:** Oh, that's easy. My favorite novel is set in Tokyo, Japan. It's *The Wind-Up Bird Chronicle* by Haruki Murakami. **A:** Um, I don't think I know that one. Is it a fantasy novel? **B:** Well, kind of … but some people say it's science fiction. It's difficult to call it a single genre. **A:** That's unusual, isn't it? **B:** Yeah, but that's the thing about Murakami. He is unusual. His novels aren't like anyone else's. He's really creative. **A:** Wow. So do you think I should read it? **B:** Absolutely!

3.2 **A:** Hey, what are you reading right now? **B:** This excellent novel. It's called *The White Tiger*. Do you know it? **A:** Um, I don't think so. Who's the author? **B:** Aravind Adiga. **A:** Aravind Adiga? Is he still alive? **B:** Oh, yes. He was born in 1974. He's still alive. **A:** Is he an African novelist? **B:** No, he's from India. All of his books are set there. He lives in Mumbai. **A:** So what's the book about? **B:** Well, it's about a lot of things, but the main character, Balram, wants to escape being poor. He does something terrible, but I'm not going to tell you what it is! **A:** Wow. Sounds interesting. Will you lend it to me when you finish reading it? **B:** Absolutely.

3.3 A lot of people I know like historical novels.; Most of the time he reads romance novels.; None of Amy's friends like science fiction.; A lot of authors work long hours.

3.4 Native speakers often drop the /v/ sound in *of*. However, if the word that comes after *of* begins with a vowel sound, then the /v/ sound is usually pronounced.

3.5 **1.** A lot of people have started reading fan fiction.; **2.** I enjoy sci-fi stories, but I like thrillers best of all.; **3.** Some of my friends joined a book group.; **4.** None of our children likes to read.; **5.** There's a box of books on the table.; **6.** If you hear of any events, let me know.; **7.** I spend most of my money on books.; **8.** Most of the time, I read romance novels.

3.6 My favorite pastime is reading. I read all the time, and I don't stick to a particular genre; I like reading all types of novels. I generally ask friends and family members for recommendations, and I also use reviews to help me decide what I'll read next. For this reason, I was glad to find Tony Miller's three reviews today. I thought his short analysis of each novel was very interesting. I mean, he provided just enough information to give you a real sense of each book. Actually, I've already read one of the novels. I read *Anya's Ghost* last year, and like Tony Miller, I was very impressed by it. In fact, I usually recommend it to people who want to give graphic novels a try. I was kind of disappointed that Miller wasn't more enthusiastic about *Gray Mountain* … I usually like everything by John Grisham, but I might avoid this one. I've decided I'm going to read *Fahrenheit 451* first. It sounds fascinating!

4.1 **1.** Hi, my name's Linda. I recently heard a new song on the radio. I have no idea who it's by but it was really loud and dark and had a very spooky sound to it. It's definitely not going to be one of my favorites.

2. I'm Mark. I just started taking music lessons from my next-door neighbor. She's trying to help me to sing better. The problem is I don't like her taste in music. She likes easy listening, which to me is so boring.

3. Hi, I'm Susan. I went to an amazing concert last night. It was an electronic band and they had this really cool rhythmic sound. It made me feel really energized so my friends and I went dancing afterward.

4.2 **A:** I made a playlist for tomorrow's party. Do you want to take a look? **B:** A playlist! That's a great idea. I'd love to see it. Oh, I love that band. And I see you have my favorite song on here. But I think there are too many hip-hop songs on your list. Not everyone is into hip-hop, you know. **A:** Yeah, that's true. **B:** I don't see any heavy metal here. **A:** Well, I actually hate heavy metal. That's why I don't have any. **B:** That's too bad. I kind of like heavy metal. How about electronic music? Did you include any? **A:** Oh yes, I've got a lot. I want people to dance at the party. Parties with no dancing are boring, don't you agree? **B:** Absolutely!

4.3 music; relaxed; audience; romantic

4.4 **1.** attitude; **2.** nostalgic; **3.** passion; **4.** rhythmic; **5.** reduce; **6.** energized; **7.** keyboard; **8.** performer

4.5 composer; spooky; musical; instrument; gentle; musician; effect; classical

4.6 Running and music go hand in hand. With this in mind, there is a new device on the market called a smart trainer. It's a headset that can store music—about 4,000 songs—as well as GPS technology and a heart monitor.

With the smart trainer you can listen to different training plans, such as cardio or fat burn. Based on your speed and heart rate, the "coach" will tell you to slow down or speed up. It will then motivate you further by playing an appropriate song for you.

I like all the technology in the smart trainer—it's more than just a music player or smart watch. The coach feature is a great idea. And I like that it chooses a song just for me. So what didn't I like? Well, I'm not sure the ear is the best way to measure heart rate. And right now it only chooses music from my own collection. It would be nice if it could suggest songs from other sources. Overall, it's an interesting new device I'm sure many people will want to have.

5.1 **A:** So did you decide which car you want? **B:** Um, I think so. Let me show it to you online … here, look. **A:** This green one? **B:** No, the black one. There. **A:** Oh that one. That is nice! **B:** Mm, I guess so. **A:** You don't sound very sure. **B:** Well, it's a really big decision. **A:** I know. But it looks like a great car. I like the contrast between the colors on the outside and inside. **B:** Yeah, that's pretty cool. And the texture of the seats is amazing, very soft leather, you know? **A:** Wow, sounds great. I also like the curved lines at the front. It's a beautiful design. **B:** Ah, that's the design element I don't like! **A:** Really? But straight lines aren't possible there … **B:** No, I know. I just mean it looks a bit too round for me. **A:** Right. So, are you going to buy it? **B:** Umm … I might. I don't know …

5.2 A shield is in the middle of the coat of arms. There is a black border around the shield. A large key and an arrow are crossed in the center of the shield. The bottom of the arrow is on the left, and the bottom of the key is on the right. Above the shield, there is a crown. There is a lion to the left of the shield, and another one to the right of it. There is a banner below the shield.

5.3 The contrast and colors make it an exciting design.; It must be difficult to work with him.; It rained all afternoon.; The patient asked for another pillow.

5.4 **A:** Kim, sorry, I can't find the design plans. **B:** I think Bob might be using them. **A:** Right. Can you ask him to send them to me, please? **B:** Oh, … I just found them, but the latest changes haven't been made yet. **A:** Great! Can you add the changes and email them to me right away? **B:** Sorry, I'm just about to go into a meeting. **A:** That's OK. It can wait until the afternoon. **B:** Sure, that should be no problem. **A:** Great. As long as I have them by the end of the day. **B:** No problem. You can depend on me!

5.5 **1.** The background color of my country's flag is blue.; **2.** I really like the red and green stripes on this flag.; **3.** This is the most beautiful flag I've ever seen.; **4.** It's only the second time I've seen this flag.

5.6 **A:** What did you think of that article about the Olympic flag? **B:** Eh … it was good, I suppose. **A:** Good? I thought it was great! **B:** Sorry. You know I'm not interested in sports. **A:** Yes, but the Olympic Games are about more than sports. **B:** Um, I don't understand. What do you mean? **A:** OK, I mean it's this huge event that brings people together, people from all over the world. **B:** Right. That's true. **A:** So that's why I love the Olympic flag. **B:** Because of the symbolism? **A:** Well, yeah, because the flag reminds us that we're connected to so many other countries! **B:** I guess it is a pretty cool flag. **A:** It's really cool! I mean, the world has a lot of problems, but the Olympics are one good thing that we can all share. That flag includes billions of us; it represents us. **B:** You know what, I think you're right. **A:** Of course I'm right!

6.1 There is someone very close to me who is a big inspiration. It's my best friend Kevin. He's amazing because he always seems to have time for everything. For example, he does a lot of volunteer work. I sometimes say I want to do that too, but don't have the time. But he says to just do it—you find the time for things when they are important.

Another person who is inspiring to me is Katie. She works next to me and we sometimes have lunch together. She is always making birthday cakes for parties and wants to start a side business. Well, she asked me to join her in selling them. Cool, huh? I really admire her for doing something she loves and for taking risks.

And then there's George. He lives next door. He's a painter and he's really good. I don't think he sells a lot but he's doing what he loves. Well, I started painting too and showed him some of my work. I was really nervous and felt like quitting. But he told me to keep painting. He thought I had a lot of talent.

6.2 My grandmother is a huge inspiration to me. She always gives me great advice. I remember I once had a part-time job that I hated. I wanted to quit but was afraid of not having a source of income. When I asked my grandmother for advice, she told me to quit my job. I was really surprised. I expected her to tell me to stick with it but she said, "Follow your passion and find something you love."

Another time she came to watch me play soccer. I missed a really easy goal. After the game, she didn't say, "That's OK. It's just a game." Instead, she said, "I know you could have scored that goal. You just need to practice more."

My grandmother also never encouraged laziness. One hot summer day, my brother and I wanted to go to the mall and we asked her to drive us there. She just said, "Have fun at the mall. Walking is good for you."

My grandmother never fails to encourage me. She's a very special woman and I love her very much.

6.3 In 1995, J. K. Rowling completed the first Harry Potter book.; Despite their best efforts, the students performed poorly.; They had a long marriage, but it was not an easy one.

6.4 **1.** After she climbed Mt. Kilimanjaro, she decided to run the London Marathon.; **2.** As a child, his older brother was a great role model.; **3.** My Aunt Janet led a very traditional life, but I found her very inspiring.; **4.** In 2016, athletes from all over the world competed at the Rio Olympic Games.; **5.** I handed in my project, but I wasn't satisfied with my work.

6.5 **1.** In 1994, my family visited the Grand Canyon.; **2.** In my opinion, teaching is a great job, but teachers don't make a lot of money.; **3.** My father always said, "As long as you've put in your best effort, you can be proud of yourself."; **4.** The three most important qualities in a hero are bravery, caring, and humility.

6.6 **A:** This blog is really interesting. It's by a woman named Kathy Caprino. **B:** I don't think I know her. **A:** She's a writer and trainer, and is interested in what makes someone inspiring. Several years ago, someone asked her who inspired her. Sadly, she answered no one. **B:** I find that hard to believe. She couldn't find one person? Not one? **A:** I know, right? But it got her thinking and she started looking at the traits of inspiring people. She found 13 traits, but she says there are three that she considers most important. First, inspiring people show bravery by setting their own path. **B:** What do you mean? **A:** They're not afraid to try new things or change the direction of their lives. Others may criticize them or not believe in them, but it doesn't matter. They just follow their hearts. **B:** That makes sense. Not many people have the courage to change—since most find change a scary thing. **A:** You're right. Second, these inspiring people focus on helping others. They feel satisfied when they spend their time helping other people. They feel good when they can contribute to someone's success. **B:** That's good. It's really important to think of others instead of yourself. Everything seems to be a race these days and people are so selfish at times. No wonder people with this trait are so inspiring! **A:** That's so true. And third, Caprino says that inspiring people are also amazing storytellers. This means that they have a unique way of looking at the world and sharing things through powerful stories. They're able to reach us emotionally through their personal stories. **B:** Yeah, I can see that. If they are bold enough to try new paths and go on new adventures, I'm sure they have plenty of stories to share!

Credits

Photo Credits

Cover © Patrick Bingham Hall, **3** Thomas J. Abercrombie/National Geographic Creative, **9** Joel Sartore/National Geographic Photo Ark/National Geographic Creative, **11** Anne B. Keiser/National Geographic Creative, **16** Compassionate Eye Foundation/Jasper White/DigitalVision/Getty Images, **18** Thomas Ernsting/laif/Redux, **23** (tr) © Macmillan Publishers, (cl) © Doubleday 1995–2016. All rights reserved., (cr) © Simon & Schuster, Inc., **25** Fairfax Media/Getty Images, **30** andresr/E+/Getty Images, **32** Jessica Espinosa/Newscom/Notimex/Ciudad de Mãxico/Distrito Federal/Mãxico, **35** (tr) Lourens Smak/Alamy, (cl) petch one/Shutterstock.com, (bl) Arcady/Shutterstock.com, (cr) Vitezslav Valka/Shutterstock.com, (br) Vitezslav Valka/Shutterstock.com, **36** Marta Jonina/Shutterstock.com, **37** Gerry Yardy/Alamy Stock Photo, **39** (tl) Everett Collection Historical/Alamy Stock Photo, (tr) Martin Shields/Alamy Stock Photo, **40** Stockbyte/Getty Images, **44** Bill Frakes/Sports Illustrated/Getty Images, **46** AP Images/Brian Lawless

Text Credits

16 Adapted from “May of Human Migration”: genographic.nationalgeographic.com